Adventures
Of a
Trapper

Adventures Of a Trapper

Written by Victor Serhienko

iUniverse, Inc.
New York Lincoln Shanghai

Adventures Of a Trapper

iUniverse books may be ordered through booksellers or by contacting:

iUniverse
2021 Pine Lake Road, Suite 100
Lincoln, NE 68512
www.iuniverse.com
1-800-Authors (1-800-288-4677)

Because of the dynamic nature of the Internet, any Web addresses or links contained in this book may have changed since publication and may no longer be valid.

The views expressed in this work are solely those of the author and do not necessarily reflect the views of the publisher, and the publisher hereby disclaims any responsibility for them.

ISBN: 978-0-595-47219-2 (pbk)

ISBN: 978-0-595-91502-6 (ebk)

Printed in the United States of America

Contents

vi   Adventures Of a Trapper

Chapter 17. 87

Chapter 18. 90

Chapter 19. 94

Chapter 20   Healthy Recipes 98

About the Author

I was born and raised on a farm on the banks of the North Saskatchewan River in Saskatchewan in September 1926.

In October 1947, after the harvest was completed, the future looked bleak job wise.

Someone noticed an ad in the weekly paper that International Nickel Company of Sudbury was hiring workers. Wage rate was eighty-two and a half cent per hour on surface and ninety-two and a half cent per hour underground.

A group of six, including myself made our way to Saskatoon where we met the Inco agent, got hired and was issued railway fare to Sudbury, Ontario.

The plan was to return home in the spring. In April, all except for me returned home. I decided to wait a little longer.

In 1950 Verna Slobodian arrived in Sudbury to be a bridesmaid at her older brother's wedding and that's where we met. In 1951 Verna attended another wedding, this time as a bride. We raised three daughters. I remained employed with Inco in various job positions until January 1982, when I accepted an early retirement package and put away my tools I used as a diesel mechanic.

I had no plans or goals for the future. It seems that there was a master plan for my life and things just kept on happening.

About the Book

I have no formal training as a writer, so I'll just write about my experiences of trapping in trapper's language.

This book has a little of everything in it. How I started hunting, information on trapping, fur bearing animals, pelt preparation and some of my adventures on the trap line. Some good, some bad, some happy, some sad and some downright stupid on my part. I've also included some of my favorite recipes that are delicious and also healthy.

Through out this book, I keep using the word "I" and it is used for want of a better pronoun. It would be more appropriate to use the word "we", because there is a Higher Power or God with me. This book has nothing to do with religion, but that the help is there when I need it. Without it, by laws of nature, I should be a forgotten memory instead of living to write about it.

I've enjoyed writing my book and sharing some of my experiences through out the years. I hope I can help some people understand that trappers are not cruel individuals, we do well for the environment and trapping is a job, like any other job.

The opinions expressed in this book are mine and mine alone.

Acknowledgements

First of all, I would like to thank my wife Verna for all the years of support she has given me. She comes every spring to make the cabin fresh and give it a good cleaning. Prior to getting electricity at the camp she would help me prepare meals for me to take. Most of all I want to thank her for being my fishing companion while I took breaks from working and especially for warning me of the snakes.

In the writing of my first book, which somehow went missing, I would like to thank my daughter, Linda and my granddaughters for their help and time that they put in typing and the printing of that copy. Even though it was not read by anyone I appreciate what they did for me.

I want to thank Susan, my youngest daughter for all the hours she put into the typing of this copy. Upon completion she was proud to hand over my manuscript to me.

Again I want to thank the above mentioned people because without them this book would not have been possible. It would have still been a thought in the back of my mind, but now it's a dream come true.

Fur Bearer photos courtesy of Fur Harvest Fur Management manual published by Ontario Trappers Association and Ministry of Natural Resources.

1

First Deer Hunt

I had done some trapping as a boy growing up in Saskatchewan. Mostly weasels, jack rabbits, squirrels, skunks and coyotes.

My Dad was a trapper. Our house was built on the edge of a huge ravine, sloping down to the river. The river was visible through the window for about a mile in each direction.

In the late fall, Dad would go by boat to trap locations on sand bars that were wind swept and had no snow build up in the winter. He would dig in the sand and place a block of wood in the shape of a trap in the hole.

In the winter, he would go to each location, lift the block of wood out and place the trap. The set was baited with lure.

Every morning he would take out his telescope and check the sets. If there was a coyote caught in the trap, he would hitch a team of horses to a cutter, drive out and retrieve the coyote.

When I started working for Inco in Sudbury, I had other interests and didn't do any trapping or hunting, until 1957 that is. One day a co-worker, Rudy asked me to go deer hunting with him. I was reluctant to agree, saying that I didn't have a gun, skills or a license. Jim, another co-worker offered to lend me his 30.30 Winchester, saying he won't be using it that weekend. Rudy offered to supply me with ammunition; all I had to do was buy a deer license, which cost five dollars at that time. So they talked me into it.

Saturday, early in the morning we left for Nairen, about forty miles west of Sudbury along Highway 17. We arrived at the parking place, it was just breaking daylight.

We walked on old overgrown road for about two miles, coming to a meadow about a quarter of a mile long. There was an old dilapidated building on each end. On the north side of the meadow there was a ridge running east to west parallel to the meadow. The ridge was covered with birch, aspen and tag alders. Rudy said to me, "You go down to the end of the meadow, climb the ridge and stand on watch. I'll start on this end and walk towards you, I might scare something up".

I arrived at the spot as directed and settled down to wait. Soon I heard a shot from the direction Rudy was at. There was a sort of a thud in the sound, similar to a bullet hitting flesh. I waited, expecting Rudy to call, but all was quite.

It was a beautiful, crisp November morning with the sun just rising. There was no snow on the ground. Shortly after I heard leaves rustling, then I saw two deer trotting towards me. I opened fire, to excited to aim properly. When they were about thirty feet away, I saw one drop. I kept shooting at the other deer till I ran out of shells. I watched the other deer vanish into the brush.

I walked over and saw a huge buck lying on the ground. I called to Rudy. All I had was a dull pocket knife. When I tried to cut the deer, the blade bent back and I cut my hand. Soon Rudy arrived. When he was finished butchering the deer I said to him, "We got our deer, let's go home". He said, "No, it's only eight o'clock, let's hunt a while longer, I might see the one that got away".

He gave me more shells; a total of nine, I think it was eight in the tubular magazine and one in the barrel. He told me not to go too far from the deer so that no one steals him. I walked back and forth a short distance, going to look at the deer to see is it was still there and not my imagination.

I sat on a rock facing north looking at the swamp. I felt hungry, so I ate a sandwich I had in my pocket. I also felt cold, so I thought I'd walk around. Just as I stood up, two deer jumped out of the brush at the bottom of the ridge and leaped across the swamp. I opened fire, even when the deer were in the water; in my excitement it never occurred to me how we would retrieve the deer, had I been lucky enough to bag one. I kept shooting till they crossed and started up a fairly steep hill. By then, they were about four hundred yards away. I could barely see them. As I fired the last shot I saw one stop, standing broadside. I wondered why the deer stopped when they were going full speed. As I looked I saw the other one sliding down the hill. With my last shot I had hit the deer and that's why the other one stopped.

At that distance there was no way I could claim good marksmanship. It was simply blind luck, a winning lottery ticket. I shouted for Rudy again. When he arrived, we walked around the swamp to the spot and found a big doe lying there. After butchering her we dragged her to where the buck lay.

It was only ten in the morning and we had our two deer. We also had a big problem. How are we going to get the deer to the car?

I stayed back with the deer. It was decided Ruby would go back to Nairen Center to see if he could find a vehicle that could drive to the kill site. Four by four pickups were not yet invented. He was fortunate to find an army jeep and late in the afternoon they drove up to the area where I was with the deer. We loaded the deer on the jeep, drove to the car and reloaded.

It was about five o'clock when we arrived in Sudbury. Rudy wanted to enter our buck in the "Big Buck Contest", as he looked big enough to qualify.

When we arrived at the Frozen Food Locker, I inquired about the cost of cutting, wrapping and the locker rental. I thought the cost too high, all we wanted was to enter the contest. The man was peeved that we had turned down his services, but reluctantly hung the deer on the scales.

It was dark by then and getting close to six o'clock. The man told us it weighed two hundred pounds and that he had bigger bucks entered already. Neither Rudy nor I looked at the scales. I was anxious to get to the beer and liquor stores before they closed. So we didn't enter. We had to ask for help as the two of us couldn't lift the deer back on the front fender of the car.

Later the butcher that cut up the deer told us we had two hundred pounds of meat from that buck. Add the weight of the head, hide and legs, it looked like we had a winner in the contest. I was bitten by the hunting bug.

The next season I purchased a 30.30 Winchester at Simpson Sears. I also booked my vacation in November for deer season.

Opening day was Saturday. We went to the same area. We hunted all day without seeing any deer. Sunday was the same. Monday, Rudy took the day off from work, no luck again. On Tuesday, I went hunting by myself as Rudy went back to work.

It was a sunny crisp day with no snow on the ground. While walking in the bush, I heard leaves rustling and saw two deer near by. It was the first and only time I developed buck fever. I emptied the gun, nine shots. I don't remember aiming. When I tried to reload, my hands were shaking so bad, the shells were flying all over till the box was empty. I spent half and hour looking for shells on the ground, some I never did find.

We went every weekend with no success. I shot at some, but missed. Finally one Saturday, I was walking in a cedar swamp. It was a mild cloudy day with large snow flakes coming down. There was about two inches of snow on the ground. Suddenly I saw a deer running towards me. I cocked and aimed the gun waiting for him to stop. At about fifty yards he saw me and stopped, facing me. I shot; he wheeled around and leaped away to his left in a semi circle. I fired two more times and he was gone.

Walking over to where he stood, I saw blood on the snow to the right side of where he was standing. Following his tracks I saw lots of blood pouring out.

About seventy-five yards away, I found him lying on the ground, dead. I had aimed for his chest but the bullet hit him in the right side of his head. He could only see out of his left eye, that's why he ran in a semi circle.

I didn't know where Rudy was, so I decided to take the deer out myself. I found two small poles curved on one end. Tying sticks across to form a make shift stretcher, I loaded the deer and lifting one end, dragging the other end I made it out.

When I got to the car, I found Rudy with the car turned around, motor running, and ready to go. Rudy was concerned about driving out since it was snowing and he had no winter tires on his car. We loaded the deer on the car and made it home safely.

Once we got home, we tried my gun target shooting and found the bullets hitting all over, missing the target completely at times. I wrote to the Winchester factory in the United States and they advised me to ship the gun to them collect. They replaced the defective barrel under warranty.

The deer population began to decline and the last deer I got was in 1963. I went out to the same area by myself. While walking through the bush, I came to a small hollow where a big doe was laying down. She jumped to her feet to run. I shot and she dropped.

She was much too heavy for me to handle alone, so I hung her up, hung my shirt to keep the wolves away and left. The next day I returned with my buddy and we carried her out. One thing I learned about deer, if they think you don't see them, they won't move.

One sunny day I was walking through the bush, it was dry and noisy. As I passed a thick stand of Jack Pine trees, I could hear, but couldn't see two hunters on the hillside. Their conversation was loud. Soon I came to an area of water which was too deep to cross. I decided to retrace my steps and go around the other way. As I walked past the heavy Jack Pines there was a crash beside me. I saw a big buck with a huge rack leaping away. I shot several times missing, the last shot knocked a branch off a tree.

The two hunters called down and asked what I was shooting at. When I told them they came running down and asked me which way he went and took off running after the buck. Their chances of catching up to the deer were slim to none.

Even though I passed the buck within ten feet, he didn't move figuring I didn't see him but when I came back, he got scared and he took off.

In the mean time, my affair with the bottle became more serious and hunting wasn't as important anymore, so the gun stayed in the case.

2

A Higher Power

My life had become so unmanageable; I realized I had to do something about it. I asked the Higher Power for help, as I could not do it on my own.

It was August 16, 1971, about ten o'clock in the morning. I was walking in a drift six hundred feet below surface at Frood Mine, when I admitted that alcohol was my problem. I felt a sensation like water being poured into a glass vase. I felt it rising from my feet upward. When it reached the top of my throat it overflowed and I felt at peace.

Like the paradox, we surrender to win. The bottle and I parted way. I lost the addiction to alcohol, both mentally and physically. It was then I discovered God, nothing to do with religion, just a Higher Power helping me when I need help. Thinking back, the Higher Power was with me all along, though I didn't realize it.

I can recall an incident when I was fourteen years old. I had been hunting jack rabbits for their pelts. At that time, a pelt was worth one dollar, which was a fortune in those days. It was November and it was cold but no snow. Rabbits were white and were visible for a long distance on the black summer follow. I used a twenty-two caliber rifle, but in some cases the rabbit would spook before I could get close enough. I switch to a sixteen gauge shot gun, I could get them on the run.

One day I bagged a jack rabbit, since they weighed about five pounds, there was no point in carrying it home when all I needed was the pelt, so I hung it up on a tree, skinned it and put the pelt in my packsack and left the carcass on the ground. A few days later wile passing by the same area I decided to make a trap set for a weasel using the rabbit carcass as bait. I found the rabbit carcass where I had left it. I gave it a kick with my foot but it was frozen solid to the ground (that hurt my toes). I took the shot gun by the barrel and tapped the carcass with the butt. There was a shell in the barrel but the gun wasn't cocked, all of a sudden there was a blast and the left side of my face went numb. I took off my mitten

5

and ran my hand on my face to see if there was any blood and thank God there wasn't. I didn't realize that the firing pin was loose in the bolt and that hitting something solid with the butt would jar the firing pin and cause the gun to explode. I never told Dad about that incident.

Another incident to prove the Higher Power is still with me. Early in my trapping career I was trapping bears. 1985, I made a snare set along side the trail to camp. I placed a foot snare on the ground. I arranged the brush, roots and branches hoping to direct the bear to step on the snare.

One morning as I drove my three wheeled *ATV* (All Terrain Vehicle) to the area where I set the snare and hoping to catch a bear. Near the snare set I noticed two black animals cross the trail, one large and one small. After taking a second look I realized that it was a mother bear and her cub.

Once checking the snare set, I saw that the snare was sprung, but no animal in the trap. As I was resetting the snare, I heard a strange noise, one I never heard before in my life. I looked up and there was the bear cub about ten feet away scolding me for being to close to what he considered to be his food. I pulled my hand gun out and fired three times and missed. He turned and disappeared, then I heard the mother calling to him and all was quiet after the call.

The next morning upon checking the snare set, I found the cub in the snare. I had shot him in the head, laid him down and reset the snare set to try and catch his mother. He was too little to damage the cable. I placed him on the *ATV*, turned around and went back to camp. Previously, a taxidermist had asked me, if I ever caught a bear cub would I bring it to him. I brought him this cub and he paid me fifty dollars for it.

I couldn't say how long after killing the bear cub, whether it had been hours; days, weeks or months did I realize just what I had done. I knew a mother bear can be very dangerous and will attack to protect her cub. Had the mother bear attacked me I know I would have been dead. The twenty-two magnum hand gun I carried was not much protection against a mother bear, unless I was lucky enough to hit the brain. There would have been no chance of starting the A.T.V. and out running her. Why did she not attack me when the cub was making noise or when I was resetting the snare trap? Why did she not attack when I shot and took her cub away? I believe my Higher Power was with me, protecting me from her. Even to this day when I think of what could have happened to me and really should have happened, I begin to sweat.

3

The Moose Hunt

In 1972, Verna, my wife, had a niece that was living in Kenora, Ontario, which is close to the Manitoba boarder. Since deer were plentiful and I had a place to stay, I went there for deer hunting. It was successful and worth the miles I drove to get there because I came home with two deer.

While shooting, I notice the rifle sights and the target were a little blurry. Someone had suggested to me to put a scope on, but the thirty-thirty was too short to mount a scope.

Back home, I went to a sporting goods store and in exchange for the thirty-thirty and a hundred and seventy-five dollars in cash, I became an owner of a 308 semi automatic, with a scope. I felt proud, seeing as on my first deer hunt in 1957, I had to borrow a rifle and shells. The salesman had assured me that the scope was sighted in and good to go hunting with.

Moose season opened in the Kenora area in September and my nephew Bill invited me to come and hunt with him and of course I was there.

Bill had a scope mounted on his 300 Savage, which the salesman, where he bought his gun also assured him that the scope was sighted in and ready for a hunt.

One evening after supper, Bill had suggested we go to the gravel pit, set up targets and check our guns to make sure that they were sighted and ready to shoot. I personally thought that it would be a waste of ammunition and time since we were both told that the guns were sighted in, but Bill insisted that we go, just to make sure. Once at the gravel pit, we set up targets three feet by three feet. I was first to try my gun. I fired a round and missed the target entirely. Bill fired his gun with the same results. It was obvious to us that the salesmen knew nothing about the scopes being sighted in. Bill and I each used a box of shells before we had our guns on target.

Bill worked for a forestry company during the day, so we had to wait for the weekend to go hunting. Since I was just sitting around while he was at work, Bill had suggested that I go by myself, drive the bush roads and possibly get lucky enough to shoot a moose. Bill knew the area very well and drew me a map where I could go and scout the roads.

The first morning when I was about twenty-five miles from Kenora, driving very slowly down a bush road, I heard a crunching noise from the rear of the car. I had a 1970 Plymouth sedan. Unsure what the noise was, I thought it wise to turn around and head back to Bill's place. As I neared town the noise grew more intense. I barely made it to the garage, only to find out the diagnosis was rear differential problems. To elaborate a three eights inch cap screw came loose and fell into the gears causing major damage to the vehicle. The garage did not stock the parts needed to repair the car and with a labor strike in transportation, it was not known when the parts would arrive. I was stranded without a vehicle and not willing to sit around till the weekend when Bill was off. The next day I rented a big *LTD* Ford, seeing as how I planned to be in the bush for several days and sleeping in the car. That day was unsuccessful. The second day it started to rain, which is not good for hunting because you can not hear the moose walking. I drove back to Kenora and returned the rented car.

Saturday morning was nice and sunny. Bill was not working so we hopped in his Toyota pickup truck and headed down a bush road looking for moose. Bill noticed some fresh moose tracks on the road. He got out of the truck and erased them with his boots so if any other hunters came by they wouldn't know that there was a moose nearby. Back in the truck, we drove a short distance. Bill stopped the truck, pointed and said "you go up the hill". We were both surprised because where he was pointed a cow and a calf were standing about one hundred and fifty yards away. I inserted the clip and was ready to shoot. While Bill was still loading his gun, he said "wait for me and we'll both shoot at the same time". Once he was ready it was decided that Bill would shoot the calf and I would shoot the cow. We both fired at the same time and the moose started to move. We fired again and then they were gone.

We both kept looking at the area where the moose had been, disappointed that we both had missed them when to our surprise again, we spotted antlers just below where the cow and calf had stood. At the same time we both fired two shots and missed. We walked up the hill to the spot where the moose had been, looking around we found the cow a short distance away laying dead. Bill walked back to the truck and drove around the bend. He saw the calf running towards the truck, he got the calf.

After field dressing both animals, we backed the truck up to the calf. We were able to load it in one piece, but with the cow being so big we had to cut it in half and drag it the short distance to the truck.

We were back in town for lunch. After lunch we started on the moose. The day was hot and the temperature was around eighty degrees and big green flies were buzzing all around. We were working in Bill's carport because it was shaded from the sun and a little breeze went through it. Bill covered the cement floor with a sheet of plastic and we lay the meat down, covering it with plastic to keep the lies off.

There was a wild game cooler in town, but it was closed due to the fact that the owner had an unfortunate fatal traffic accident a few days before. None of the butcher shops would handle the wild meat due to health regulations.

That was my first moose, so I knew nothing about caring for the meat. Bill had shot moose years previous to this and should have known better. In the evening we removed the plastic cover to turn the meat over. In doing so we both noticed a disturbing odor. The next morning when we went in the carport to check the meat, the odor was definitely undeniable. Bill stared cutting and wrapping his share of the meat to put in the freezer.

I was nine hundred miles away from home with a pile of meat starting to go bad and a disabled car in the garage with no parts to repair it. The only option I had was to rent a car to get the meat home before it spoiled. I rented the same Ford *LTD* that I had earlier in the week, lined the trunk with plastic, and loaded my share of meat. After putting several bags of ice on top, I closed the lid and started the drive back to Sudbury. We were long on luck but short on brains.

I drove through the night arriving in Sudbury Monday morning. At the butcher shop when I opened the trunk lid the smell was anything but pleasant. I was sure the meat was all spoiled. However the butcher with his knowledge managed to save a substantial portion of the meat. The smell was so bad in the shop, the butcher had to burn string to deaden the odor.

After he finished cutting the meat I brought it home and Verna, my wife and I spent the rest of the day wrapping it. Not knowing any better I then piled the entire packages one on top of the other, therefore the outside of the meat froze but the center did not.

The smell in the trunk of the rented car after transporting the meat home was absolutely intolerable. I used several cans of air freshener, boxing soda and drove all the way back to Kenora with the trunk lid partially opened. I brought Verna and my daughter Susan along for the ride.

Being such a big car, the *LTD* was a real gas guzzler. Past Thunder Bay I had put off filling the gas tank a little too long. It was fall and got dark early and there wasn't that much traffic on the Trans Canada highway at that time of night. It was getting late and the service stations were closed. The gas gauge showed empty when I finally got to a gas station that unfortunately was closed, but being at a closed gas station was better than being stranded on the highway.

I parked with the parking lights on and we tried to get comfortable assuming we would be there till the station opened. Shortly and Ontario Provincial Police cruiser notice the car at the station and came to check way we were there. Upon learning of the situation I had got myself into, he offered to drive me to the next opened gas station so I could at least get a five gallon jerry can of gas. We then got to the opened station, filled up and continued on our way to Kenora.

We arrived in Kenora early in the morning. Upon returning the rented car, I was elated to find that I only had to pay fifty-one dollars for the car. There was a daily charge and no fee for mileage, which was great because we are looking at over eighteen hundred miles. We had to stay until the parts for my car arrived. In the mean time we had a great visit and were headed home by the weekend.

If only I knew then what I know now, I could have saved myself all of work, time and expense. I learned all we had to do was to hang the moose quarters in the shade, rub vinegar and sprinkle black pepper all over the meat to keep the flies away and keep the meat fresh until the membrane dries. After when the membrane dries, you peel it off before eating the meat.

In 1979, my pal Leo and his brother Rosaire invited me to a fly in moose hunt. Each hunt kept getting more exciting. We flew in from Sunset View Camps that were located near Chapleau Ontario.

When we arrived at the lake where we planned to camp, we saw from the air a narrow swamp about a quarter of a mile from the lake. There were lost of trails crossing the tall grass, which was an indication of moose signs.

After we set up camp, we thought it would be a good idea to check out the swamp. Using a compass, we blazed a trail to the swamp. The moose signs we saw from the air were right on, there were lots of fresh moose tracks all over. It was decided that I would go watch the swamp while Leo and Rosaire would paddle the canoe up the creek. We then went back to camp to have lunch and to get our gear needed for our hunt. We set out late in the afternoon, Leo and Rosaire with the canoe and I with a cushion and a flashlight. After reaching the swamp I made myself comfortable behind a small spruce tree at the edge of the clearing. I settled down patiently waiting for a moose. To make a moose call you use an "URRR" sound instead of a "MOO", keeping it as long and loud as you can. I made a call every fifteen minutes or so, but all was quite. It started to get dusk, so I decided to head back to camp. Just as I stood up I heard a branch snap to my right. Then a slurping noise, that of a leg being pulled out of the mud. I took a step forward and looked around the spruce tree and saw the big black outline of a moose. I aimed and fired. A long streak of flame came out of the barrel blinding me for a second. I saw the moose moving away. Firing two more shots, I lost sight of the moose and all was quiet.

It was totally dark at that time of season. It gets from dusk to dark in a matter of moments at this time of the year. Leo and Rosaire having heard the shots came over. Using the flashlight we looked around the area where the moose had been standing. We found a large pool of blood, but there was little we could do as it was dark. We decided it would be best to return in the morning.

In the morning after breakfast, we headed back to the location where I took shots at the moose. During the night there had been a heavy rain fall. Upon returning to the site all signs of the blood had been washed away by the rain. The only sign of blood we found was on a leaf that we turned over.

It looked hopeless with all the tracks; we couldn't make out which ones to follow. There was no snow on the ground because of the rain the night before. Leo said he would take the canoe and go hunting. With all the blood I thought the moose to be mortally wounded and wouldn't go far. Rosaire and I started walking through the bush alongside the clearing. Rosaire was talking in a loud voice when I heard some noise up ahead, so I asked him to be quiet. I came out into the clearing and saw a moose standing broadside about one hundred and fifty yards away, I aimed and fired. I lost sight of the target for a second due to the kick back of the gun. I was ready to fire again but I could not see the moose. Looking at the spot where he was standing I saw water splashing and legs kicking. I had dropped him with the first shot. I started walking towards him bust soon came to water too deep for my boots. Seeing a beaver dam to my left that I could use to cross over I started walking next to the swamp. I didn't walk very far when I came upon the cow I had shot the evening before. She didn't go very far before she dropped. Rosaire came out of the bush and we field dressed the cow. Using the beaver dam we were able to get to the other side where we found the calf. After the cow is shot the calf will stay near by for days. We field dressed the calf and then the real work began.

After taking the hide off, we cut the animals into quarters. We made a stretcher by taking two dry slender poles with short sticks tied across. Loading a quarter at a time it wasn't hard taking them out, one man in front and one in the back. Meanwhile Leo having heard the shooting came over to give us a hand.

Though we hunted for the rest of the week, we did not see any more moose. The rest of the time was spent fishing and let me tell you the pike were plentiful.

4

The Fur Industry

The development of the fur trade began in the 1600's. As explores moved west through Canada, beaver pelts for the fashionable hats soon became the most sought after fur.

In 1670, the Hudson's Bay Company was granted exclusive fur trading rights for all land draining into the Hudson and James Bays. There was fierce competition among the trappers. Several trappers worked the same choice areas and took as many animals as they possibly could. The pelt has no value in the summer due to the thin hair. They start to grow long and thick fur with the onset of cold weather. In October, that is when they begin to get fuller coats. To get ahead of others, some trappers started too early, thus not getting full value for their pelts. Due to over trapping, the population of the beaver began to decline. There were few regulations and law enforcement was very minimal.

Between 1916 and 1945, Ontario began to develop control of its fur resources. Through new laws, licensing, restricted harvests, controlled seasons, royalty payments and the protection of the beaver habitat, the beaver population began to grow.

Theft of animals from traps was very common. In the 1930's, in the far north there was an incident where a trapper named Albert Johnson was accused of theft. When the Royal Canadian Mounted Police went out to investigate, they were met with a hail of bullets. In the following manhunt on snowshoes and dog sled, four Mounties were dead before Johnson was shot himself. Later there was a song recorded on a 78 *rpm* record of the story of Albert Johnson.

In the late 1940's, all crown land, with the exception of parks was divided into registered trap lines. Trap lines consisted of one or two townships, depending on the location, terrain and animal habitat. That system virtually eliminated all the problems. One trapper was granted exclusive trapping rights to one trap line. It was in his interest to manage the animal population, not to over trap or under trap and to leave enough breeding stock for reproduction.

Quotas are set with the idea of keeping the population stable. Beaver quotas are usually one beaver per live house. Forty live houses equal a quota of forty beaver. The trapper must harvest at least seventy-five percent of his quotas. There is danger in under trapping because the beaver numbers increase and food and space shortage develop.

A beaver family consists of the parents, this year's kits and last years yearlings, which help care for the kits. The second year the yearlings look for their own territory. Beavers are very territorial. They build a lodge and mark their boundary with castor scent. Strange beaver are not tolerated and driven out.

A beaver must have a suitable location, water deep enough not to freeze over in the winter and a nearby food supply. He must have a stored food supply to last the entire winter. If there are more beaver than territories, the beaver begin to starve and prone to infectious diseases and death.

5

Preparation of the Pelts

Animals must be removed from traps carefully. If the animal is frozen to the trap it must be thawed so not to damage the fur. They are hung to dry, and then they are brushed to remove any debris except otter, which should be kept damp to prevent damage to the hair. Any blood on the fur must be rinsed out.

The pelt is then removed. Only two species, beaver and bear are skinned open, which is cut from the lower lip along the belly to the tail. The rest of the animals are skinned cased or round. A cut is made from each heel of the hind leg to the anus. The tail must be stripped, that is bone pulled out of the fur except for the otter. Those must be skinned out.

Pelt removal must be done with care. Contact with fat damages the fur. Nicks and cuts to the skin must be avoided. The pelt is then cleaned and scraped of fat and flesh.

Cased pelts are put on a proper sized boards, the bottom is pinned to the board. The pelt should not be over stretched as that will thin the fur and not under stretched because that will make the pelt smaller and wrinkle. A wedge is inserted between the belly and the beard. The pelt shrinks as it dries. Absence of the wedge would make it impossible to remove the pelt.

Pelts marketed with fur in stay on the board until dry. After they are removed, any fat remaining on the pelt is cleaned, visible hair brushed. Pelts marketed with fur out stay on the board until partially dry then removed and turned inside out and put back on the board to complete the drying process.

The pelts must be turned at the right time. Turned too soon, the skin will begin to rot against the board. Turned too late and the skin will tear while turning, particularly delicate pelts such as marten. It is through hands on experience to know the right time to turn them. Fur in pelts includes red squirrel, weasel, raccoon, mink, muskrat, otter and skunk. Fur out pelts is fisher, fox, lynx, marten, coyote and wolf. After the drying process is complete, the pelts are removed from the boards and fur brushed for a neat appearance. A well handled pelt brings in more money. The pelts are hung in a cool place until shipped to the auction sale.

Beaver are nailed to a plywood drying board. There are seven oval patterns marked on the board. The pattern that fits the size of the beaver is used; again the pelt must not be over or under stretched. The fat and flesh are cleaned off the skin. Blood is then rinsed off with mild detergent and warm water. After drying the pelts are taken off the boards, removing any remaining fat, cleaned off and fur brushed. They are then stacked fur to fur and leather to leather ready for shipping to the auction.

The fur is picked up by truck at various locations all over Central and Northern Ontario. North American Fur Auction of Toronto and Fur Harvesters of North Bay provide this service. Four or five auction sales are held each year, the first usually held in December. At the warehouse, the pelts are graded by size, color and fur texture. Each pelt is assigned the trappers identification number.

The fur out pelts are put in huge drums containing sawdust and slowly rotated. This process cleans the fur to be ready for tanning. Pelts are sold in bundles. Each bundle contains identical pelts. Buyers from around the world attend the sale and bid on their needs. After the sale the fur is shipped to the tannery, where it is processed into leather. It is then shipped to furriers that purchased them to be made into coats, trim and various other items. Some beaver is sheared (long hair cut off), then dyed. I have seen a coat made from beaver that looked like purple velvet.

From the gross proceeds of the sale, deductions are made for the following:

1. Fur pickup.
2. Drumming. One dollar and fifty cent per pelt.
3. Provincial Royalty, which is five percent of previous year's average.

For example, if the average price for a marten was fifty dollars, the royalty would be two dollars and fifty cents and

4. Eleven percent commission.
5. The remainder is sent to the trapper.

6

Trapping

Through scientific research and development, great improvements have been achieved for more humane trapping. Quick killing conibear traps and power snares are now used to eliminate suffering of animals.

The old type leg hold trap has been banned except in drowning sets and soft padded jaws for lynx, fox and wolf. A drowning set is a trap set in water near shore. When a beaver gets caught he dives into deeper water but can not surface because of the slide lock on the anchor wire. The stored oxygen in his lungs runs out and the beaver dies without any pain.

The traps with soft padded jaws do not injure the leg of the animal. The sets must be checked daily. On rare occasions a trap or snare will misfire and does not kill the animal outright. But as a whole the animals suffer more in their daily lives than through trapping.

There is a misunderstanding by the public about trapping due to wrong and lack of information. Unless we see things with our own eyes we must rely on information about issues or events from what we read or hear from the media or on TV.

Those against trapping and hunting flood the media with knowledge about how animals suffer great pain in traps and should be left alone. On the surface it makes sense but let's look at the facts.

The animal kingdom is one huge food chain with the smallest being food for the larger animals. When God created life he included pain and suffering. Man has learned to lessen pain to some degree but the animals suffer in silence. Except for rabbits and beaver the rest of the animals are carnivores and will eat anything they can bring down. Some will eat their own species.

When wolves bring down a moose, usually by ham stringing the hind legs, therefore the moose is unable to move. The wolves start to feed on the choicest cut, the hind quarters, while the moose is still alive. That is suffering; the anti-groups cannot blame the trapper or hunter for that.

17

Animals in the wild lead a hard life filled with stress and pain. From the day they are born they are at the mercy of predators. About fifty percent of the young do not reach their first birthday. They are under constant stress in searching for food and not becoming food themselves. There are even waterproof fleas that live in the beaver's fur in water. Often I must spray the beaver fur with Raid before skinning it to get rid of the fleas.

Here in Northern Ontario there is an abundance of black flies and mosquitoes which appear in early spring and last till late fall. Anyone not familiar with these insects, consider yourselves very thankful. Be it human or animal these flies are very aggressive and will crawl on the body, including eyes, ears, nose and start biting and sucking for blood. That creates and unbearable itch, humans can scratch or apply anti itch medication. Imagine the agony the animal suffers, especially moose and bear with their thick hair. The moose will rub against a tree or rock to relieve the itch; at times hard enough to rub the hair out and break the skin, leaving the sores open to infection and possible death.

Many animals, including moose and bear, seek open areas to avoid the flying insects. A significant amount of the animals will wander onto the highways and are killed by vehicles. Many people are also killed at the same time because this usually happens at night when the flies are at there worse. Moose and bear are dark in color and at times there is no warning of them being on the highway and weighing hundreds of pounds, there is no contest at time between them and the vehicle.

Let us look at the life of a moose. From the day it is born, approximately the month of April, it is under great pressure to watch for wolves and bear and also endure those pesky insects. If it is fortunate enough to last till fall, another hazard is added, the hunter. If the calf survives the fall hunt more hardship is added, deep snow, intense cold and searching for scarce food buried by the snow.

After celebrating its first birthday, the fight for life continues. The anti activists believe the animals should be left alone so they can happily scamper and frolic in the forest, living their lives quietly and pass on of old age. Facts and statistics prove otherwise. Nature is hard and cruel, going from one extreme to another, from having an over abundance to extinction.

Some years ago at a park in Southern Ontario, the deer became over populated, creating a food shortage. The Ministry of Natural Resources planned a controlled hunt to reduce the herd to a tolerable level. The anti groups protest so vigorously and loudly that the Ministry back down. The deer in their starved weakened condition developed a contagious disease and the herd was wiped out inhumanly. There was not a single deer to be seen. The activists got there way and the deer died in a much crueler way than if they were hunted.

Over population is also damaging to property. In the late 1990's such was the case in Ipperwash Park located at Grand Bend in Southern Ontario. The deer wandered onto roads and into populated areas in search of food. My granddaughter's car was totaled in a collision with a deer. Again I thank my Higher Power that she was not hurt, only shaken. Even though she drove below the speed limit, being aware of the deer situation it was something that was unavoidable because of the over population.

They also destroyed gardens and the farmer's crops. There was an incident where a deer walked through a picture window of a trailer at a family trailer park, believing he saw his reflection in the window thinking it was another deer.

There was a controlled hunt in the area that year. The deer herd is kept at a sustainable level. All life requires proper nutrition, space and light for a healthy state of survival. When you walk down a trail in the woods, you can observe a tree five feet from the trail with branches reaching into the trail for space and sunlight.

A lesson can be learned from plant life. Scatter some vegetable seeds in the garden and they will grow. Nature throws a few weeds in the garden and the vegetables become weak and slow in growth. Pull the weeds, thin the vegetable plants so that they have enough space and nutrition and you end up with hearty, healthy vegetables.

Such is the case with animals. Surplus animals must be removed in order to have a healthy population. The anti activists certainly are entitled to their beliefs but when it comes to destroying property and endangering the lives of people, it's being pushed a little too far.

At one time in England, anti groups attended a mink ranch and opened all the doors to the cages. The "freed" mink having been raised in captivity had no knowledge or instinct of how to live life in the wild. Many of the mink became victims to predators; many were run over by vehicles on the roads and many of the mink died of starvation because they did not know how to hunt for prey to survive. While in captivity the mink were fed regularly, had warm, dry living conditions and no fear of predators. Clearly what these activists did without the knowledge of what would happen to these caged animals, failed in that display of good doing and ending up killing most of the mink.

Other actions taken by activists are spraying paint on fur coats worn by people is not sane or rational. Activists have to right to force their beliefs on others. People should have the freedom to make a choice of what they want to wear.

The anti groups put out information that is sometimes not always accurate. In some cases the information is incomplete and biased in their favor. For instance, in 2006 The Timmins Times, a local newspaper published a letter that was addressed to The Editor. The letter was about trapping, that it was not a renewable resource. The writer went on to point out the error of that statement, saying once an animal is killed, how could it possibly be used again?

One of the definitions in Webster's Dictionary for the word renewable is, replaceable. Be it forestry, animal or plant life, replacements re harvested. He supplied this e-mail address so that he could enlighten the public. Clearly he is an anti trapper.

7

Animals Common in Northern Ontario

Black Bear

The black bear is common to forested areas and is not found in the south or the far north of Ontario. They look larger than they are due to their thick fur. Male's weight is two hundred and fifty pounds and females one hundred and forty pounds.

Black bears lead solitary lives except at mating time which takes place between June and August. Bears have a delayed implantation. If the summer food supply is low and the females is unable to store enough fate reserves to produce young the egg will abort

Bears hibernate in dens from the end of October to March. The female bear gives birth in late January. She will deliver one to three cubs that weigh approximately six to nine ounces. Within two months the cubs increase their weight by one thousand percent due to the mother's rich milk. The cubs climb trees easily in case of danger. The female breeds every second year because the young stay with their mother for sixteen months.

A bear can't trot like most animals because it is pigeon toed. As the bear starts galloping the front paws will straighten out. It is interesting to note that the bears shed their foot pads during hibernation.

Male bears will kill small cubs if given the chance. The mother bear must be extra vigilant. A mother bear is most dangerous when she is with her cubs.

There is a demand for bear gall bladders in Asia, where the price is thousands of dollars a gram. The gall bladders are used for medicine or aphrodisiac. Bears gall bladder sales were legal but they were banned in the early 1990's to eliminate bear poaching. I received one hundred and forty dollars for one gall from a large bear.

When bears emerge from hibernation their food consists of green grass and tender leaves from trees to get their digestive system going. They will eat anything they can find. They will root in rotten logs for worms or other insects. Given the chance they will kill young moose or deer. They are also experts at catching fish. Berries in season are their main food, and of course like Winnie the Pooh, black bears really love honey.

Beaver

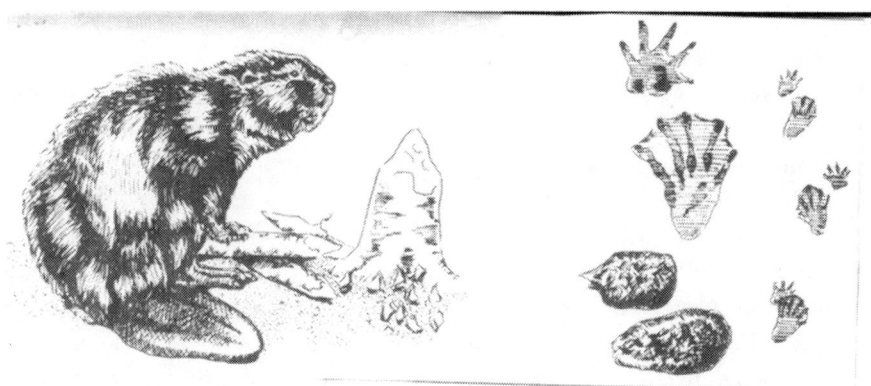

The beaver (Castor Canadensis) gets the first part of its scientific name from the castor glands under the skin between his hind legs. This occurs in both the male and female. This semi aquatic fur beaver was of great significance in the early exploration and settling of Canada. Because of its key roll in Canadian history, the beaver has become a national emblem depicted on coins, stamps and souvenirs.

Native to Canada and the United States the beaver is found where ever there is water and deciduous trees. The beaver appears clumsy on land but is agile in water. Its scaly paddle shaped tail is used for swimming and diving, to signal alarm and to kill.

The female produces her first litter at the age of two or three. Breeding takes place in water between January and March. The gestation period is one hundred and ten days. The size of the litter depends on the females age and food supply. The average litter consists of three to five kits. The beaver family consists of the parents, kits and last years young which help to care for the kits. By late summer the yearlings leave for their own territory.

The beaver are accomplished engineers, building dams from sticks, stones and mud. These dams are difficult to tear apart, therefore making them good homes. They build dams in running streams, causing the water to back up increasing depth and surface area. The flooding which results allow the beaver to fell (cut) trees which were formerly too far from shore. The beaver pond provides habitat for a variety of species including ducks, muskrats, mink, otter, moose and deer. Some beaver ponds support speckled trout.

Beaver will create ponds by building a dam on a small stream. On several occasions while traveling on my trails, I came to a pond where there was dry land before. The stream of water was hard to see but they built a dam and water back up to flood the area.

The beaver are very territorial. They mark their boundary with castor scent. They will attack other beaver that trespass. Their lodges are built in a conical shape from sticks and mud with a hole on top for ventilation. They maybe surrounded by water or against a bank.

In late September the beaver begin to create a food supply for the winter. They cut trees and branches, drag and pile them in front of the lodge, from the bottom to the surface of the water. When ice appears on the water they stay in their lodge. They dive through the tunnel and bring back some sticks to eat the bark off. The white sticks are taken out and dropped on the bottom of the pond.

The beaver's metabolism goes down as they are not as active during the winter. Their favorite food is the bark of aspen trees; however they will eat cedar, maple, alder and roots under water in the summer.

Like rabbits, beaver practice coprophagy, the eating of their own droppings. This allows the digestive system to extract all of the nutrients from the wood. Beaver gnash their top and bottom incisors together so that their teeth, which are constantly growing are kept worn down and sharp.

The beaver are safe in the water but are vulnerable on land when they fell trees. Wolves and bear have the advantage because they live on land. I have trapped numerous beaver with holes in their pelts from wolf teeth when the beaver won the battle.

Along with the pelt, the castors are also harvested and dried to be used by the perfume industry.

Otter

The otter has along slender body with a thick layer of fat beneath the skin. Adults measure between thirty to fifty inches, nose to tail. They weigh between ten to thirty pounds. The tail is wide at the base and tapers to a point at the end. The otters coat is short, rich and glossy. The fur is dark in color, varying from black to brown.

The otter mate during March and April. The gestation period is from nine and a half months to a year. Litters average two to four in size.

Otter live close to water but do not build houses, but live in burrows or old beaver houses. They are constantly on the move traveling over lakes, on land to another waterway. It takes about a week to complete the circuit.

The otter's food consists of mainly fish and any other edible species they can find in the water.

They usually travel in numbers and are very playful, diving and sliding down banks.

The otter is the most difficult of the fur bearers to skin. When dry the hair is easily damaged so the fur must be kept wet when skinning. The tail has to be skinned out; the bone cannot be pulled out as other animals. Some trappers do not trap otter because of the difficult fur preparation.

Muskrat

The muskrat is a member of the weasel family. It gets its common name from the musky odor produced by the two scent glands in the anal region of the male.

The most common and widely distributed fur bearer on this continent, the muskrat contributes greatly to the North Americas trappers. The muskrat is an aquatic animal that lives in the water. It has a flattened tail to assist in swimming and has flaps that close nostrils, ears and mouth for underwater feeding. A muskrat can store enough oxygen to stay submerged for fifteen minutes.

Weighing about two pounds, they mate in early spring. The gestation period is thirty days. The average size of a litter is four. A female can produce up to four litters per year.

Their food consists of roots, stalks and underwater plants. They will also eat frogs, crayfish and muskrat carcasses.

They live in houses similar to beaver houses but only smaller and made from grass and mud. They also frequent beaver houses and are often caught in beaver traps set at the entrance to the house.

Mortality rates are high due to the many enemies which include mink, fox, wolf, lynx, owl and hawks. Because of the multiple litters during the year, the population remains constant.

Muskrats are sometimes referred to as the poor mans mink. Their fur somewhat resembles the minks though the mink has shorter hair.

Mink

The mink has short legs and a long slender body. It is dark brown in color and weighs about a pound and a half to two pounds. A semi aquatic mammal it has dense, oily under fur for protection in the water. It has defensive musk glands which give off an offensive odor.

The male and female mink are capable of mating at ten months of age. A number of mates maybe taken by the male and female during the mating season. They mate between late February and early April. The usual gestation period is fifty-one days. A female may give birth to two to ten kits, but on the norm, its usually four.

In April or May the young are born in dens lined with grass and leaves. Their eyes open after about twenty-five days, and weaning occurs within five or six weeks after birth. They grow very fast, females attaining their adult weight at four months and the males a seven to ten months.

Mink spend as much time in water as on land, therefore they are found nears streams, lakes, ponds and rivers. The mink will eat almost any living thing it can over power. Often they fall prey to larger animals. Its diet consists of fish, cray-fish, clams, mice, earthworms, insects, frogs, muskrat, moles, rabbits and birds.

Mink are also raised in captivity on ranches. The fur on the wild mink is much better on the mink in captivity.

Marten (a.k.a. Sable)

The marten has a long slender body, a small head with a short, pointed muzzle, large rounded ears and dark brown eyes with a long bushy tail half the length of its body. Males weigh an average of one and half to two pounds. Females average one to one and a half pounds. The color norm is a golden brown that may vary from yellow to nearly black. There are spots on the throat of a mink that could vary in color all the way from an orangey to white. The prime fur has a soft rich texture, except in the summer when it becomes thin and coarse as guard hairs and much of the under fur are shed. New growth begins in late summer and is completed by October.

Marten are solitary creatures except in mating time when they can be seen in pairs. They breed during July and August often mating with several partners. There is a delayed implantation as the gestation period lasts only twenty-seven days. The kits are born during March and April and the average litter consists of three.

Marten prefer to inhabit large tracts of mature coniferous and mixed wood forests. They can travel through the tops of trees as fast as they do on the ground.

Den sites include hollow trees, under logs, stumps, rock crevices as well as squirrel nests.

Marten prey on birds, insects and small mammals. Their diet can also include rabbits, squirrels, chipmunks, carrion (dead carcasses) of various kinds and fruit. They are attracted to smelly carrion.

Their soft silky fur is in great demand for fur coats.

Fisher

Fisher is a member of the weasel family. The name is deceiving as the fisher rarely goes into the water.

The fisher's wedge shaped head is set on a stout neck. It has short heavy legs, sharp claws and a long bush tail. The male weighs anywhere from eight to twelve pounds, measuring thirty-five to forty-seven inches, from nose to tip of the tail. The females average in weigh from four to six pounds, with a length of thirty to thirty-seven inches.

The pelt ranges in color from grey-brown to black. It is lighter on the sides and darker towards the rump and tail. The face, neck and shoulders are often heavily frosted with grey or pale brown. A few white patches are found on the neck, throat, belly and the inner part of the leg. The adult males fur is fairly coarse and grizzled while the females is lighter and silkier. During spring and summer the fur becomes lighter in color and less dense. By November the fur is dense and glossy and prime. It is no longer at peak prime ness after late January.

Breeding begins in March or April, a few days after the birth of the young from the previous years mating. Fisher has delayed implantation, breeding fifty-one weeks before the kits are born. Active pregnancy lasts only eight weeks. The average litter contains three kits. The kits nurse for about 4 months and begin to eat meat before they are weaned.

Fisher is adaptable animals that will live in a variety of forested areas, so long as there is something to eat. They avoid open areas, preferring dense forest of mixed conifers and hard woods. Hollow trees and logs, holes in rocky ledges and old porcupine dens are likely den sites.

The fisher eats what it can find, anything from rabbits, small mammals, grouse, small birds and their eggs, amphibians, fish, insects' fruit and nuts. Carrion is also consumed. It is especially noted for preying on porcupine, which it kills by repeatedly attacking the face and head. I have trapped a fisher that had a porcupine quill embedding in his testes. Now that's pain.

Except for brief periods during the breeding season, fisher leads solitary lives, traveling extensively in search of food. They usually remain on the ground but can climb trees and swim if necessary.

The female pelt being softer and silkier is in more demand than the males.

Raccoon

The raccoon is famous for its bushy tail with the four to six black rings, its sparkling black eyes and the black mask over its eyes, nose and cheeks, which gives it the look of a mischievous bandit. Its skull is broad and its face tapers from the short, rounded white tipped ears to the button like nose.

The adult male measures thirty-seven to forty-seven inches from nose to the tip of the tail and weighs an average eighteen pounds and the female about sixteen pounds.

The fur consists of a brown wooly undercoat with long guard hairs which are white tipped on the belly and flanks and black tipped on the back. The coat ranges in color from black to tawny pale grey or white.

Breeding takes place between January and March. During this time the male travels as much as fifteen miles a night in search of a mate. The male may take more than one partner during the mating season.

Following a sixty-five day gestation period, the young are born between mid April and mid May and the size of the litter maybe one to six, the average being three. Born blind, they are able to climb trees with their mother to escape danger even before they can see. Their eyes open at three weeks and at six weeks they are ready to leave the nest. By two months of age the young are able to forage for food with their mother.

Their habitat is forested areas near water. They live in hollow trees, logs or burrows. Raccoon could also be found in urban areas and can become a nuisance when it nests in farm buildings. The omnivorous raccoon eats young birds, bird's eggs, small mammals, carrion, poultry, fish, frogs, shellfish, insects, fruit, nuts, berries and corn. The raccoon has a habit of washing its food before eating it if water is available. At temperatures below freezing the raccoon remain in their dens until it warms up. This is not true hibernation, since they will emerge from their dens on warm days in the winter.

Skunk

The skunk is a cat sized animal with two white stripes on the back of its black coat and down the bushy tail. It has a small head with a pointed snout which allows the skunk to poke into jars, cans and holes in search of food. It has short legs and is slow and awkward in moving. In defense it sprays a yellow foul smelling liquid for as far as ten feet. Despite the spray, fisher, fox and wolves prefer skunk in their diets.

Skunks breed between late February and late march. The gestation period is sixty-three days and the young are born in May. The size of the litter is six on the average.

Skunks prefer open country side. They are not found in dense forests but are tolerant of urban activity and can live in cities.

A large part of their diet consists of beetles, grubs, and grasshoppers. Small mammals are included in their diet along with turtle, bird eggs and vegetables.

The skunk has habit of digging holes in lawns and gardens in searches of insects make it a nuisance to land owners.

Lynx

The lynx is lean and stout in body. It has long muscular legs and large feet with toes that spread to give it extra mobility in deep snow. Its black tipped tail is very short and blunt and its tufted ears are long and triangular. It has prominent eyes and a broad blunt nose. Ruffs of hair form sideburns along its cheeks. The lynx's long haired coat is a pale grey with brown streaks. The guard hairs are white at the base, darker in the middle and black at the tips.

The average adult male measures thirty-five inches and the female slightly less. The average weight of either sex is seventeen pounds. Although the lynx does not reach its full size until two years of age, it can breed during its first year.

Breeding takes place in late winter, between January and March. After mating the male does not remain with the female. However, when the kittens are born sixty days later he may return to help provide food. From one to four kittens are born between March and May.

Weighing ten ounces, the newborn are furred and are blind for the first ten days. They are weaned at two months of age and begin to venture outside the den. The family remains near the den for three months, by which time the female has begun to teach the young to capture mice. Later when their skills improve they will prey on rabbits.

The primary food of the lynx is the snow shoe hare. It has been estimated that one lynx can consume about one hundred and seventy rabbits per year. In times of shortage the lynx also prey on grouse, waterfowl, squirrels mice, chipmunks, skunks, porcupines, eggs and fish. Carrion may also be eaten but plant matter is rarely consumed.

The lynx population corresponds to that of the rabbit population. Lynx give birth to fewer young when rabbits are scarce. At such times the young seldom live beyond their first year. Many adults also die when food is scarce.

In 1985, the rabbit cycle was at its lowest, therefore so was the lynx. The lynx season closed all through Northern Ontario for several years. During that period the top price for lynx was fourteen hundred dollars. The season has since reopened with an abundant number of hares and lynx.

Red Fox

About the size of a miniature collie dog, the fox looks larger than the dog due to its long hair and bushy tail. It stands about fourteen inches at the shoulder and is roughly thirty-seven inches in length. Males weigh ten to fifteen pounds, with the females weighing slightly less.

The long silky coat is burnished orange or golden yellow, with a darker shade of rusty brown along the back. The ears are white inside and black outside. The legs and paws are black. The long bushy tail has a white tip.

By early December the male begins to wander in search of a mate. Breeding takes place in late January or early February and the pups are born in March or April, after a gestation period of fifty-two days.

In Northern Ontario the average litter size is six, while in Southern Ontario the average is eight. The newborns are blind and deaf and weigh about four ounces. The pups are weaned at two months. This allows the vixen to join her mate in the hunt for food. Gradually the pups begin to accompany their parents on hunting trips. In late fall the young begin to disperse.

The red fox prefer mixed terrain and does well in farming country. Ideal habitat consists of open fields, rolling hills, river valleys and forest edges.

Although the red fox is considered a carnivore, it will eat almost anything. Its diet consists of small mice, groundhogs, muskrats, rabbits and carrion.

When hunting the fox trots back and forth as it traces rodent scent with its keen nose. When the prey is located, the fox stands motionless with one paw raised and its ears directed towards the sound. It then springs, landing with its front paws on the prey. Larger prey maybe ambushed or chased by several foxes at one time. Leftovers are often cached in dirt, snow or dry vegetation for later use. The red fox is also fond of skunks.

Wolf

Wolvers are common in Northern forests and not found in Southern Ontario. It is the size of a large German Shepard, but is legs are more lanky and its chest narrower. It has a large frame and a broader forehead.

Males weigh from sixty to eighty pounds and Northern wolves maybe even heavier. Females are lighter by ten to fifteen pounds and have smaller frames. The average wolf stands between twenty-four to thirty inches at the shoulder and measures between forty-eight and seventy-five inches from nose to the tip of the tail. The wolf's front feet are larger than its hind feet, but both sets are large and provide mobility on snowy terrain.

Fur color varies, pelts range from white to coal black. White is common in the Arctic and black in the Algonquin region. The wolf usually wears a grizzled grey coat. The dense fur around the neck is tipped in grey or black. The legs and belly are buff colored and the large bushy tail is tawny on the underside and tipped with black.

The female is sexually mature at two years of age and the male at three years. Each wolf pack has only one breeding pair and this couple dominates the other members. Mates remain together for life. Breeding occurs between late February and mid March with the young being born in early May after a gestation period of sixty-three days. The average Ontario litter contains five pups. The helpless newborns are blind and their eyes open within the first ten to twelve days with weaning at six weeks to two months. They begin to eat regurgitated meat provided by their attentive parents. The milk teeth lost at this time are gradually replaced by permanent teeth during the first year of life.

The wolf prefers forested habitat with high vantage points and clearings, but it can also live in hilly, craggy places or in areas offering a mixture of forest and open countryside. It is usually found in close proximity to water. Den sites include hollow logs, caves and underneath tangled roots. The dens have two entrances and face south.

Wolves will eat anything they can bring down. While their preference is beaver, caribou, elk, moose and deer, they will also eat rabbits, muskrat, raccoon, mice, otter and lynx. They usually kill domestic livestock when other foods are in short supply. In the summer vegetation and fruit are added to the diet. The animals are heavy eaters consuming up to one fifth of their own body weight at one time.

Wolves prey on beaver when the beaver is on land to fell trees. Young deer and moose are taken are brought down. Wolf packs will bring down an adult moose by tiring the moose by following and harassing it. Then they surround him while some keep snapping at his face and others cut the tendons on the hind legs. When the moose is down the wolves begin to feed on the still alive moose.

The average pack consists of six to ten members. Within the pack they are very social and maintain a class system. Vocal communication usually takes the form of prolonged loud throaty howls, a lot deeper than a coyote. It is more intense during the breeding season.

Coyote

A relative of the wolf, it is also called a brush wolf in Southern areas.

The coyote is found throughout Canada, except in the boreal forest and the Arctic tundra. It has adapted well to the agriculture areas of central and Southern Ontario and are even found in the city of Toronto.

The coyote is about the size of a small collie, but has a narrower snout and nose. The average male weighs up to thirty-five pounds while the female is about thirty pounds. Both sexes average four feet in length.

Its pelt is a grayish fawn color with heavy dark tipped hairs along the back and tail. The throat is white and white patches may also be found on the chest and belly. The ears are chestnut brown and the muzzle grizzled.

Breeding takes place between late January and March. The pups are born sixty-three days after mating takes place. Litters usually contain four to six pups. The newborn are blind and weigh about eight ounces. At three or four weeks the young are able to leave the den. By August, the pups have gone on excursions with the adults and are familiar with the surrounding territory.

Coyote habitat includes the highly developed mixed farming areas further south, swamplands, parks and the edges of cities and towns.

Like the fox, the coyote eats whatever is available and will consume vegetable matter as well as meat and carrion. Its diet also consists of mice, ground hogs, rabbits, grouse and chickens if a hen house is around the area.

Like other canids coyote are active throughout the year. They are chiefly nocturnal but are active as well at dawn and dusk. They are vocal animals and are particularly noisy during mating season. Their song consists of yips, howls, warbles and barks. Their noise is a lot higher than the deep tone of the wolf.

Weasel (A.K.A. Ermine)

The weasel is similar to a mink, though a lot smaller and with a slender body. The tail is skinny with a black tip.

Breeding takes place in August, with litters being born in late spring, around late April or May. Gestation takes approximately nine months. Weasels are born in litters of six to eight and are blind. Weaning occurs within just over a month, at which time the male parent begins to bring food to the underground nest. At seven or eight weeks the young are old enough to hunt. Although weasels may live to be five or six years old, most of them will die of natural causes.

Weasels prefer woodlands, holes in stone piles or walls, thickets and fences rows. They are usually found near water and can be seen around buildings, wood piles and logs.

The weasel preys on mice, rats, voles, rabbits, chipmunks, shrews, lizards, small snakes, birds, bats, insects and earthworms. It also eats bird's eggs and will attack poultry. The weasel kills quickly by a bite to the back of the skull. It will kill more than it can eat. Back in Saskatchewan, on our farm a weasel entered the hen house and killed fourteen chickens.

Like the rabbit, the weasel changes color with the seasons. During summer it is brown and in the winter he is pure white, except for his black eyes, black tip of the tail and pink nose.

Red Squirrel

Approximately one half the size of a grey squirrel, the red squirrel weights about five to eleven ounces and measures about ten to fifteen inches, nose to tail tip.

The sexes look alike and show seasonal color variation. In summer they are rusty red on the upper body and grey white on the lower and have a black strip along each side. In winter the fur becomes paler and the black stripes disappear.

Females can produce two litters a year. Breeding occurs in late February or March, then again in June and July. After a gestation period of thirty-six to forty days, one to seven babies are born. They are naked and remain blind for twenty-seven days. At about one month, they begin to venture out of the nest and are weaned shortly after. The young disperse in late summer or early fall.

The red squirrel prefers a coniferous forest. Nests are built close to the tree trunks or in tree cavities.

In the red squirrel's diet, seeds of spruce and pine trees, nuts, mushrooms, meat, sap, young birds and bird's eggs are the norm. Food is cached in amounts up to a bushel.

Active by day or moonlit nights, the red squirrel is a chatterer. It clucks grunts and calls out warnings. The red squirrel is a solitary creature, except during mating season.

The red squirrel is agile in trees and can jump five feet outward and three feet upward from a moving branch. The red squirrel is also known to be a good swimmer.

8

I always thought that life would be great if I didn't have to go to work. On the last week in January of 1982, my wish came true. I took an early retirement package from Inco and didn't have to work any more.

It didn't take long to realize that the grass wasn't greener on the other side of the fence, it wasn't even green. I missed the routine of going to work and my co-workers. I started to worry that I had made the wrong decision to take the early retirement package.

In early spring while browsing through a catalogue of night courses at the local college, I noticed one that caught my attention, which were Fur Harvest and Fur Management. The long dormant interest in trapping came awake after reading what the course entailed. After some research, I found the course was mandatory to qualify for a trapper's license. It didn't take long to decide to enroll.

In May I completed the course and received a diploma that made me eligible for a trapper's license. After receiving the diploma I soon found out there was a catch and that was, that I had to have a place to trap to be able to obtain a license. To my disappointment, I soon found out that there were no vacant registered trap lines available and trapping on private line was not economically feasible. I filed applications for a trap line in Sudbury, Gogama and Chapleau, but again, only to find out that no lines were available.

In January of 1983, my buddy Leo, who lived in Val Caron, told me of a trapper on his street thinking of giving up his trap line. I quickly went to his home, but his wife informed me he was out on the line and she expected him back in a week. What a long week it was for me.

When he returned, I went to see him and was pleased that we soon were able to agree on a price. I would purchase the cabin and equipment only, not the ground the cabin sat on because that was Crownland and came with the trap line. A five dollar trapping license would make me a 01 trapper on the trap line.

Since the trap line was in the Gogama area, I had to see the Ministry of Natural Resources in Gogama about getting the trap line transferred to me. There I was told there were previous applications filed for trap lines. They would go over all applications to see who was more qualified. The trapping lines were awarded on the point system. Points were earned for … how far away the applicant lived

45

… what equipment he owned … whether he completed the trappers course … and whether he was a member of a Trappers Council.

There were some anxious moments; finally I received a call from the Ministry of Natural Resources, informing me that I didn't have an application on file. I was upset to hear that, knowing that I had filed one. Shortly after receiving that call I received another telling me that they had found my application and that I had enough points to qualify to get the trap line.

In the first week of March, Henry, the former owner of the trap line journeyed to Gogama and signed papers for the transfer. I paid five dollars, was issued the license and finally was the 01 trapper on Go #23 and on probation for a year. The manager at the time, Jack offered me a small beaver quota so I could trap till the end of March. I turned him down; next fall would come soon enough.

My trap line consisted of two townships, a township being six square miles, which meant I had seventy-two square miles of ground. It was eighty-five miles North of Sudbury, along Highway 144 to Sultan Road, then fifteen miles by logging roads. Eddie Forest Company was harvesting logs on and around my trap line. It was good and bad. The good part was that I had roads to access lakes and ponds and the bad parts was they destroyed animal habitat.

The cabin was an old building constructed out of logs. Henry had made some repairs, put in a new floor which made it snug and warm.

He kept the outboard motor and gas tank under his cot. The firewood pile was outside covered with snow. He would shovel snow off the wood pile and bring some logs inside and put them in the oven to dry so it would burn.

I wanted more room so I decided to build a shed. One weekend in late March, Henry, Leo, Ray and I went up to camp to start the shed; we cut and hauled enough logs to build it. While there we did some ice fishing and caught some pickerel and a twenty pound pike.

I had to park at the end of the road and use a skidoo trail for one and a half miles to get to camp. The winter trail was fine, but in the summer it was full of mud holes and very rough. I had purchased and 1983 All Terrain Vehicle, a Big Red. Leo and I built a two wheeled trailer to haul our supplies. We kept getting stuck in the mud holes, so it was a must that they be filled some how. There was a lot of work and time filling the holes. It is a constant job and after twenty-four years of work, it's still rough, but passable without getting stuck.

In early May, Leo and I went to peel the logs for the shed. We had a difficult time; the bark seemed to be glued to the logs. Had we cut the logs in May instead of earlier in March, the bark would have peeled away easily, but if we would have waited till May, we would have had no way of hauling the longs to camp because in March we brought them to by skidoo.

We finally finished peeling the bark we had planned to build the shed with. We had the logs standing on end, about two inches apart. A one inch deep chain saw cut on each side of the log lengthwise, made it possible to slide a quarter inch plywood two inches wide in the grooves, which made it weather proof. It was slow going and there was no shortage of mosquitoes and black flies.

The trail from the truck to the camp was too rough for Verna, so I cut a shorter trail to the lake, which we walked then continued the rest of the way by boat. One weekend Verna came with me to help with the shed. We arrived late in the afternoon. The ground around the camp was covered with long grass, scrap and wood lying around everywhere.

The next morning my arms full of tools, I started for the shed. As I came around the corner of the camp I saw a snake in front of me. I screamed and ran back to the camp. I could not force myself to walk to the shed to work on it. Verna is not overly fond of snakes herself, but she took a stick and swished the grass and wood piles to make sure there was nothing around. Even then she could not convince me to go out there, remarking that I was as white as a sheet. So we packed up and headed for home.

I had wanted a trap line so badly that I had forgotten about my phobia of snakes. I just didn't think about how I would hand the situation when I saw one and I was bound to see others sooner or later. I don't know why I was so terrified of snakes. I would scream and run. It couldn't be heredity, as my dad used to pick the up with his bare hands.

Although, I do recall an incident when I was about two years of age, there was a one room log building with no foundation, just logs resting on rocks. It was summer and I was standing inside by the screen door looking out. I saw a snake crawling towards the door, it kept coming and crawled under the floor, right where I was standing. I cannot remember anything else after that, whether I cried or screamed. If I remember correctly, I was alone in the house. Perhaps that was the caused of my phobia.

My parents used to dig Seneca roots in the bush. The dried roots were used for medicine and provided much needed income. My mother used to hitch a big dog named Bob to a wagon and me being a baby at the time, she would put me in the wagon and make her way into the bush so she could dig for roots. Once there she would spread a blanket on the ground and leave me at the mercy of the black flies and mosquitoes. There is a possibility that a snake came by and caused my phobia. I just don't know, all I know is that it was ruining my life at camp.

Somehow I got enough courage to keep going back to camp. Eventually we got the shed finished and started to clear the area around the cabin of grass and debris and every other thing that a snake could possibly hide in. During this time we spent some of that time fishing and a lot of time still working on the trail to keep them passable.

9

Trapping season begins on October 15th for beaver and otter. I looked forward to this day with dread and anticipation. I was excited that I would be able to start trapping and dread because I had no idea where to start. I did not plan my runs and didn't know the area. Henry, the trapper before me promised to help me by showing me the trails, but he was nowhere about.

First day of the season, using a fourteen foot aluminum boat and a nine and a half horse power Johnson outboard motor I went to the west end of Schist Lake to make some trap sets. While in shallow water, the motor struck a rock and broke the shear pin. Needless to say being a green horn I carried no spares. So I had to paddle all the way back to camp with one oar, which was all I had. It was long and tiring, therefore making my first day, not a good one.

The trails were made for winter use after freeze up. In early fall there were mud holes to keep filling and streams to bridge. All this work should have been done in the summer, but being my first year I didn't know any better. By using the map of the trap lines I was able to locate some lakes to check for live beaver houses. I hauled a twelve foot Scott canoe, with a two h.p. Johnson motor on the trailer behind the *ATV*

One day while paddling the canoe on Bod Lake, which is close to the road, I heard the honking of a car horn. I paddled to shore and found it to be Tom, the Conservation Officer; he had been looking for me. He handed me a map of my trap line with all live beaver houses marked. The Ministry of Natural Resources had done an aerial beaver house count on my trap line. They counted forty houses, therefore making my beaver quota forty. I considered that to be a big win fall, as I doubt that I could have found that many on my own. Live houses are easy to spot due to the branches of the food pile in front of the house. In winter it is difficult as everything is covered by the snow.

There is a creek about a mile long joining Yeo Lake and Canoe Lake. There was a live beaver house on the Canoe Lake end of the creek. One day I crossed Yeo Lake and went up the creek and made sets at the beaver house. It was the end of October and being inexperienced the thought of the freeze up never even entered my mind. A few days later I went back to check the traps. Crossing Yeo Lake was no problem, but when I reached the mouth, the creek was frozen. The ice was too thick to brake with a paddle, but not thick enough to walk on. Inexperience showing again, I didn't know that I could have waited until the ice was thick enough to walk on to get the traps out. Not knowing that, I dragged the canoe while walking on the shoreline up to the beaver house. I managed to lift the traps, which by the way were empty, put the traps in the canoe and headed back the same way I came. That was another long day, but not wasted because I learned a valuable lesson. All traps set in water must be lifted by the end of October.

On October 25th the season opened for the rest of to the fur bearers, marten, fox, fisher, lynx, weasel and wolf.

When the snow got too deep for the *ATV*, I used a snow machine. I had an Alpine skidoo, a double track with one ski in front. It was difficult to drive with the both tracks, driving it tended to go straight when I tried to turn. I also had a small Snow Cruiser that was easier to drive but was temper mental and very hard to start at times.

Being a greenhorn I didn't know that the trail had to be broken before pulling a sled. One day with the Snow Cruiser towing a sled with all my gear, I started down the south trail. Because the trail wasn't broken before heading out, when I came to a hill I couldn't make it up. I back tracked and took a longer route.

After completing my run and on my way back to camp, while passing the road to Yeo Lake, I decided to check the lake. I had no traps set there to check, I just wanted to break the trail and check for animal tracks. When I reached the lake I drove onto the bay to turn around. I didn't check the bay for slush, which is water under the snow, like I was suppose to. And of course there was slush and the wet snow packed the track of the skidoo and there was poor traction. I managed to get to shore, cleaned the packed snow from the boogie wheel and continued on.

With all the detours and burning more gas due to pulling the sled the gas tank went dry. I had no choice but to walk back to camp. I packed the small animals like the mink and marten and I left the beaver on the sled. It was a four and a half mile walk back to camp and another four and a half miles back the next morning with a gas can. I filled the tank with gas and was on my way again.

On the way back to camp I met up with Henry and his brother Ben. They had come to visit me and to do some ice fishing. Once we got back to camp with their supplies, unload and had lunch we went ice fishing. They had brought a case of beer and some home made wine. Henry brought some wine when we went fishing. He kept sipping on it all afternoon. We had no luck and didn't catch any fish at all.

When we got back to camp, we set some fishing lines in the holes in front of the camp. Henry continued sipping on the wine. Soon he got to be obnoxious, interruptive and monopolized the conversations, repeating the same thing over and over. Ben got fed up and went to bed. I had stayed up late the night before skinning so I was tired, so I decided to go to bed too. Since I had gone to bed I just assumed that Henry would just sit quietly at the table, but no such luck, he sat there alone still sipping on the wine and talking to himself.

Unable to sleep, I laid in bed listening to him ramble. I heard him say something about my camp, and then he said "no it's not my camp, its Vic's, I sold it to him". A little while later he said to himself, "I think I'll go check the lines". I could hear him getting dressed, zipping up his skidoo suit and then putting on his boots. Once dressed, he sat back down at the table with his glass of wine and said, "I'm all dressed and I have to go somewhere but I can't remember where". Lying in bed I couldn't help but laugh to myself. He finally made his way out the door and started his snow machine, going out on the lake to check the fishing lines we had set earlier. He soon returned grumbling that there was no fish on the lines. He undressed, sat at the table, had a bit more wine and finally went to bed. The next morning he was up bright and bushy tailed with no sign of a hangover.

On a January morning in 1984, while checking traps I came to find some fresh moose tracks on a logging road. Since I had wolf snares set in the area, I was afraid the moose would knock them down. On my way to check them I came around the bend and was surprised to see a big bull moose standing there. He had a snare on each of his front legs. I had set a wolf snare in each rut of the road. Since the area was clear cut, there were no trees to anchor the snares to. So I cut down two birch trees about fifteen feet long and three inches at the butt and laid them along side the road for anchors. There was no way I could set him free myself and needed help.

I had to drive the skidoo ten miles to the Eddie Forest 303 camp where they had a two way radio. From there, Donna called the main camp at Ramsey, ten miles to the west of where we were. They had a telephone there and were able to call the Ministry of Natural Resources in Gogama to advise them of the situation and that I needed help with. Soon two Conservation Officers arrived, Jack and Tom. They did not have a tranquillizer gun, so they had to tie the syringe on a long stick in order to inject the moose. Their first experience trying to sedate a moose, they were unsure of the dosage the needed. Then Jack said, "Tom, Vic and I will stand in front of the moose and you go around and jab him in the rear". When the plan was put into action, the moose looked at us then at Tom, he the laid his ears back, lowered his head and tried to charge at us. The two birch trees the snares were anchored to kept him in his position preventing him from charging.

Eventually Tom was able to administer the shot. The moose stood still for a while then his knees started to tremble and soon he was lying down. We then were able to remove the snares from his front legs. There was no injury to moose as he wasn't there very long. The eyes of the moose stayed opened while he was out. The Conservation Officers were concerned about them being injured from the cold, so they covered him with blankets to protect them.

Apparently the dose was too strong because it was late afternoon when he finally started showing signs of movement again. He then got up, his legs trembling for a few minutes and then with a slap on the rump from Jack the moose was on his way with no harm done to him.

The moose had lost his rack already. Both moose and deer loose their horns in late fall. When the new rack grows in the spring a point is added, therefore making it possible to tell the approximate age by the size of the rack.

How little I knew about snow machines. On a mild day I was driving back to camp on the lake. Once at the camp I parked the skidoo. The next morning I started the engine, let it warm up, shifted into forward, but the machine wouldn't move. I then tried reverse with the same result. I didn't know what to do, so the only thing I could think of was to walk to the truck and go for help. When I put the cover on the machine, I tried to pass the hold down strap through the track. I couldn't because it was packed with frozen snow.

Could that have been the problem? I cleaned all the snow and ice that was frozen around the track, started it, put it in forward and away it went.

Another valuable lesson learned. Always clean wet snow from the track before parking for a long while or over night. Dry snow does not affect the performance of the snow machine.

One day I drove the skidoo to the west end of the lake. When I came to the bay at the end of the lake, I slowed down to turn around. As I lost speed, the skidoo sank deeper into the snow and reached slush. The track soon got packed with wet snow making the machine that much heavier. The machine sank down to the ice and the track was spinning but it being on ice there was no traction and I was going no where.

The previous trapper, Henry had given me some good advice. Always carry a shovel and snow shoes on the skidoo. I added an axe as part of my equipment along with a small rope pulley hoist. Walking on snow shoes I was able to reach shore, where I cut three poles about ten feet long and two inches at the butt. I made a tripod at the rear of the snow machine and with the rope hoist hanging from the top of the tripod; I hoisted the rear of the skidoo and cleaned out the wet snow. I then cut two dry poles about thirty feet in length and laid them side by side with the ends under the track, so when the machine was lowered it sat on the poles. I was then able to pick up enough speed to keep on going by the time I reached the end of the poles.

Another similar incident occurred when I went to check a beaver set around the bend from camp. I did not have the snow shoes on the skidoo this time as it was near to the camp and I thought I wouldn't need them. I was wrong. Near the set there was slush and the snow machine sank in the snow reaching the ice. Again being on ice I had no traction and was not going anywhere.

I had to walk back to camp in deep snow which was difficult, but fortunately it was a short walk this time. Wearing snow shoes I walked back to the snow machine with the necessary equipment that I should have with me in the first place. Once there I used the tripod and hoisted the rear of the machine out of the snow. I then cleaned out all the slush from the track and boogie wheels, left it on the hoist overnight and I the morning I walked back to get it. With the slush freezing overnight I was able to drive the skidoo back to camp.

There are many hazards to be aware of especially when I'm alone. The first winter I trapped to the very end of beaver season, which is the 31st of March. I managed to harvest thirty-nine beavers out of the forty, which was only one short of my quota.

I had kept a diary of my activities that first year. Reading it recently, made me wonder how I survived all alone. But then I wasn't really alone, I had my Higher Power with me and for that I give thanks.

10

When I took possession of the camp, there was no ceiling, just rafters. We brought in supplies, mostly carried over the short trail to the lake by hand, and then loaded into the boat. I put in ceiling rafters, plywood and insulation, which made the camp warmer in the winter and cooler in the summer. I also laid another layer of plywood to the floor.

There were three Americans from Michigan who would make a trip for fishing and loved staying at the camp; Verne, Ken and Ray were their names. They brought me a hand pump, a well point and the required pipes I needed to make it functional. I sunk the point down through the floor by the sink and had lots of fresh water. I didn't have to carry water from the lake anymore, or boil the water before drinking it.

Little by little conditions began to improve and get easier. I brought in an eight cubic foot Serval propane refrigerator and a one hundred pound propane tank. I was able to install propane lights, which was a great improvement over the old Coleman lantern I had and cook food without using the kitchen cook stove which made the camp very hot in the summer.

One weekend my daughter Susan and her husband Marc came to the camp with us. I let them have the boat, motor and fishing rods to go fishing. I was left with the canoe and an old fishing rod I found. For something to do I paddled out into the bay in front of the camp. The water was shallow and covered with lily pads. As I cast out for the first there was a big splash, and what looked like a ten pound pike took the Williams Wobbler lure. Being an old rod, the line was as old and not too strong. I had no landing net, how was I going to land him. After playing him for about ten minutes, I brought him close to the canoe where he lay on the surface.

I had an idea, as always I had my hand gun with me, you remember, for the snakes. Why not shot him in the head? I proceeded to do just that, I aimed, fired, the line went slack and the fish was gone. I reeled in the line and saw what had happened. I missed his head but hit the lure and because it wasn't solid the bullet didn't penetrate, but slid the length of the lure, making a grove and pushed the ring holding the hook out of the lure.

A lot of people didn't believe this story even when I showed them the lure with the grove down the length of it. With time the lure disappeared, I don't know where.

One day late in September, I arrived at camp late in the afternoon and the weather was cool. The aluminum boat was on shore upside down. I cautiously flipped it right side up, relieved that nothing had crawled out of it. The outboard motor and gas tank I had put on board in the dark with a flashlight. The next morning was still fairly cold, but I took a fishing rod and went out on the lake anyways.

I had lost a transducer cord in the water from a fish finder some time before. I spent some time dragging the bottom hoping to snag it, without success but I caught a pickerel while trolling. While heading back towards camp for a coffee break, the sun was shining over my shoulder into the front of the boat. I happened to glance at where the bow curves up and saw something that looked like a snake doubled up on the floor. I stood up and looked closer; sure enough is was a snake. My first impulse was to jump into the water even though I can't swim but instead I believe my Higher Power stopped me and gave me the courage to pick up and oar and pound the snake until it was dead. Using the other oar as chopsticks, I picked up the snake and tossed it overboard.

When the boat was upside down, during the day the aluminum was warm and the snake had curled itself up on the small ledge at the bow. When the weather got cold it got groggy and didn't move. When I had flipped the boat over the day before, it just fell on the floor and stayed there.

Twenty-four years later as I write about it, I just realized that I had just about stepped on it while getting into the boat. Even now thinking about it I break out into a sweat.

Verna was with me. I flipped the boat over right side up and pounded the ledge in the front of the boat with a stick learning a lesson last year. To my relief there was no snake this time. We fished for some time and caught a few pike. It was getting on towards evening and suggested that we go to shore, leave the pike in the live well and pick up some more minnows and go try for pickerel.

After doing all that we pulled away from shore and I had just opened the throttle full out when I noticed Verna stand up and take a step back, she was pointing to the front of the boat. I looked to where she was pointing and saw a long skinny snake slithering in the bow. The next thing I remember was silence. Whether I shut the motor off or it stalled from fright, I don't recall. Just like last year, I did the same thing; beat it until it was dead with an oar then chop sticked it out of the boat.

Later after looking at the boat I discovered the ledge had a curve on the bottom, creating a little trough and that's where the snake was when I pounded the ledge with the stick. To prevent that from happening again I cemented a one inch diameter rope in the trough. The salesman gave me a funny look at the hardware store when I asked for eighteen inches of rope.

A few days later I decided to try fishing pickerel in the morning, so I woke up at six a.m. Verna said it was too early for her and decided staying in bed. Upon my return, she told me of the scare she had. No snakes involved in her story. She was still in bed when she heard footsteps approaching the cabin. She hurried to lock the door from the inside thinking it might be someone trying to break in. She was surprised to see a large moose about four feet from the cabin walk by and into the bay. The moose are not as plentiful these days as they were years ago.

Once I was looking out the window and saw a cow moose with her calf in the lake about three hundred yards away. Verna was out back, so I went out to get her to see the moose. When the cow saw us she got all excited and swam around her calf. She didn't know whether she should go ahead or turn back. Before long they were around the point and out of sight. So if you hear that moose are near sighted, don't believe it because that happening proved it wrong.

With all the accessories I added to the cabin I started feeling a little crowded in there, so I decided to add an addition in the front. I built it out of poles standing upright like the shed. The plywood and shingles with the *ATV* and the old type storm windows were carried down the shorter trail to the landing and brought those by boat to the camp.

Our granddaughters, Jennifer, seven years old and Kristy Ann, four years old were visiting us and came to help us and of course all was not work. We had taken the girls fishing and were trolling. I caught a pike about twelve inches long, which is too small to keep, so I was going to release it, but Jennifer said, "no I want it, let's keep it". As I was taking the fish with my left hand it flipped and one of the several treble hooks on the lure went deep into the base of my thumb. Because of the barbs I couldn't remove the hook myself, so I had to cut the line and wearing the lure in my thumb we packed up and made our way to the truck.

We lived in Sudbury at the time so we drove the one hundred miles to get home. I went to the General Hospital Emergency room and upon entering I my family doctor happened to be there. He thought that was a big joke, but he cut the hook out and put two stitches in and told me to come back in a week to take the stitches out. We went back to camp the next morning. Jennifer blamed herself, so in a week instead of going back to the hospital she took the stitches out.

Almost the same thing happened when I was by myself. This time instead of leaving the lure on my hand, I cut the hook near the skin with a pair of pliers. By the time I arrived at the hospital the hook was not visible, it had worked itself into the flesh. The only way the doctor could find it was to take an x-ray. He scolded me for cutting the hook. He told me next time, leave the lure there, but so far there hasn't been a next time. Knock on wood.

At the shore by the cabin the water is shallow and the bottom is mud. I had problems with the boat coming in and going out. Another project for me, I build a dock. I cut and dragged logs with the *ATV* built piers and filled them with rocks. Laying the logs on top of the piers, I had a dock and that still stands today. A little askew as the ice moves things around in the spring.

11

I trapped black bear earlier on in my trapping days. My Americans friends, Ken, Verne and Ray liked the bear meat and taxidermist bought the bear hides for mounting and sale of gall bladders were legal then.

One day in May, I was driving my *ATV* on Chester Road heading to Wolf Lake to check some bear sets. As I approached a curve in the road I saw a large hawk or eagle take flight from the side of the road with a snake writhing in its claws. I watched the bird but kept driving. The bird got frightened and dropped the snake and as I watched it fall, making sure it wasn't near me, I saw it landed on a tall Jack Pine tree. When I returned from my run the bird was perched in the tree that the snake fell on.

It was raining the next day so I didn't go out, but the day I traveled the same road and I couldn't believe my eyes. Just like a video replay, from the same spot and possibly the same hawk, with maybe the same snake in his claws took flight. This time I stopped and watched the hawk fly away to have his lunch. It is just amazing to see the things that nature has to offer.

While trapping bear one spring, I wanted to try a promising spot. Since it was outside my trap line I had to have a bear license to shoot bear, not only trap. I was allowed to trap or shoot bear on my ground under my trapper's license. I baited a site at the base of a Jack Pine tree about one hundred and fifty yards from the logging road. The area was cut over so the visibility was good.

One evening I went over to watch for bear. I sat on the *ATV* parked in amongst some young Jack Pines. There was some smelly bait in a container on the rear rack of the *ATV,* so I wore a head net as the black flies were intense. Sitting quietly I watched the baited site.

First a moose walked by between the bait and me. A lynx then walked by the area looking scrawny in his summer. Neither animal was aware of me. Then for some reason I turned my head and saw a big bear about twenty feet away. The movement startled him and he loped away grumbling to himself. About ten minutes later, having circled around he suddenly appeared at the baited site. It was an easy shot with the 308 with him standing broad side.

I had read many articles on bear hunting, including the importance of wearing gloves when handling bait and not leaving human scent at the site. This bear proved them wrong, but there is always an exception to a rule.

Bears are fairly easy to trap. Once in September while on the way to brush out a trail, I came upon a spot on Yeo Road where a bear went to the bathroom and forgot to flush the toilet, so obviously he was in the area. I made a snare set in the brush beside the road. A few days later when I came back to check the trap, I couldn't believe my eyes, there was a big bear with his foot in the snare. It was the biggest bear I have ever trapped, weighing approximately three hundred pounds. I sold the hide to a taxidermist, who made a bear rug, which lies on someone's floor to this day.

In October 2005, I was on my way home towing a trailer with the *ATV* on it. About two miles out I came upon some partridge on the road. I stopped, loaded the twelve gauge shotgun and shot two. Leaning the unloaded gun on the trailer, I cleaned the birds and got back in the truck continuing on my way. More or less ninety miles later, on the outskirts of Timmins, where we now live, I happened to glance over at the passenger side and to my dismay saw that the gun was not there. I had left it leaning against the trailer. I figured there was no use going back because I was certain that the gun would have been picked up by other hunters and gone by the time I drove back.

Once I arrived home, I called the South Porcupine Ontario Provincial Police detachment and suggested to them that they should maybe call the Gogama OPP detachment, since the gun was lost in their area. Shortly after reporting the forgotten gun, the phone rang and it was an officer from the Gogama OPP. He asked me if I had reported a lost firearm and I answer, "Yes I did". Then he had asked me if I could tell him where I had lost it. I replied, "Turn right on Sultan Road from Highway 144, drive about three kilometers down the road, turn right on Chester Road, continue on for fourteen kilometer, then turn left on a side road". He told me that he would follow my directions and drive out there to see if he could locate it.

A couple of hours later the phone rang again. It was the officer that I had given the directions to earlier. He told me that he had found my gun and asked me when I planned to return to camp. I answered that I planned on heading back on Sunday, but he said he would be in Timmins before that, so he would leave the gun at the South Porcupine detachment. The next morning he called asking for my address and told me he would drop the gun off at the house. It wasn't long after that he was knocking at the door with my gun and after checking the possession certificate he gave it to me. He told me to be more careful in the future. Had it been a Conservation Officer that had found the gun he would have charged me.

There was another occasion that could have ended in disaster, but didn't. In late November 1987, I was on my way to camp towing the trailer with the *ATV* on it and there was about four inches of fresh snow on the road. Around a mile from where I park at the end of the road, there is a sharp left turn and a fairly long steep hill going down. Then at the bottom of the hill there is a sharp right turn with another steep hill going up. Usually at that of year I would park on top of the hill. If there is a snow fall, I'll have a problem making the hill as my truck was only a two wheel drive and I had no tire chains. When I arrived at the top of the hill the thought crossed my mind that I should park there, but I had made a bad decision and a very stupid one and kept on going. When I had reached the bottom and made the sharp right turn I had no room to speed up and the wheels started to spin. I backed down and tried again with the same result.

I was at the bottom and couldn't make the hill, neither up nor down. Just as I began to worry about what I should do, I looked up and saw a red globe against the white snow. It shouldn't be there; I blinked my eyes and looked again. Then I realized it was the red light up top the roof of the Ministry of Natural Resources truck coming down the hill towards me. At that time there was only once large red globe on official law enforcement vehicles.

I sure was glad to see Mark, the Conservation Officer got out of the truck and asked me if I had problems. I explained my situation and the problem was resolved in a short time. Mark hooked up my trailer to his four by four truck and towed it back up the hill. I made it back without the trailer. I parked on top of the hill where I should have in the first place.

Mark came to camp with me and we got the skidoo going which was stored in the shed at camp for the summer. We had a coffee and then he left. He said he saw fresh tire tracks and decided to follow them. Why was he in the area? The moose hunting season was over. Why did he decide to follow the tracks, luck or coincidence? I see the hand of the Higher Power again.

12

For trapping mink or marten, I use the same box. I build a box from one inch rough lumber, eighteen inches in length, with a four and a half inch square inside opening. One end is closed off with a one inch mesh wire screen. The other end has one inch slots cut in the vertical sides for the springs of the 120 conibear trap.

Starting in September, when I clean the fish I catch, I save the heads, backbone and everything else not edible and pack it in container and freeze it for mink bait.

In making a mink set, I place the box on the ground where a mink would likely pass, by a stream, beaver dam or house and then emptying a container of bait towards the rear of the box, then place a 120 trap in the front of the box and cover the box with evergreen branches to make it look more natural.

When a mink comes around, seeing as how he can't reach the bait from the screen end, he goes in the trap end and gets caught ... and sometimes not.

One time I came to check a set placed beside a creek. There was a fresh snowfall and I could see fresh mink tracks all over the area, but the trap was still in place, not sprung. I wanted to check if the bait was still in place, sometimes mice will clean it out through the screen. To look inside I would have to tilt the box. I didn't want to disturb the branches, so I knelt down and looked inside from the front of the trap end. All of a sudden there was a noise and a blur of brown fur, the trap slammed shut then flew out of the box and there laid a dead mink in the trap. Apparently he managed to squeeze its way past the trigger and was inside having lunch when he saw my ugly face staring at him and took off in a hurry right into the trap.

Another time when I checked an otter set, I found a mink caught in the 220. A 220 conibear is similar to a 120, the only difference is its seven inch square instead of four and a half in square. I placed a dry pole across the narrow creek so that it rested on the surface of the water. A 220 trap was hung from the pole in the water. When an animal swims to the pole in naturally dives under rather than go over the pole.

While I was resetting the trap, I saw another mink swimming in my direction. When I finished resetting the trap I walked away rather than follow the creek because I didn't want to scare the mink. After I had checked the rest of the sets I had in the area I then started back and when I came to where I had seen the mink, I saw he was in the trap, dead. I took the mink out and had to reset the trap again, not complaining.

If conditions are favorable with the water being deep enough near the shore to be able to make a drowning set, I make a double barrel set. A 120 conibear trap is set inside the box and one and a half inch leg hold trap is set in the water in front of the box. The mink caught in the leg hold will slide down on the wire to the bottom and the other will stay in the 120 trap.

I once checked a mink set by a creek and saw a large male mink eating the mink that was in the trap. Lots of animals will eat their own species. I reset the trap and caught the mink, but the eaten one was damaged and wasted. That is why it is important to check the sets often because the pelts could be damaged by other animals or mice.

WATER LEVEL

SLIDE LOCKS

1½ LEG HOLD

.20 CON BEAR

ROCK

DOUBLE BARREL MINK SET

In making of marten sets, I use the same box but place it off the ground or on a tree vertically or horizontally. Bait is usually beaver or other carcasses. Marten are attracted to stale, smelly bait. When a marten gets caught in a trap he will hang where the mice can't get him.

It is important to anchor the trap solid, you never know what animal can get caught. For example, I once made a marten set on a Jack Pine tree about ten inches in diameter. I nailed the box to the tree in a vertical position. I didn't want to waste wire to go all around the tree to anchor the trap, so I drove a two and a half inch nail into the tree, put the trap chain on the nail and to make a somewhat hook, I bent it. That anchor was solid enough for a marten. When I checked next time out, the trap was gone, it some how had slipped off the nail. There was loose bark at the base of the tree and there were signs of a struggle with the trap in the snow. The tracks disappeared on a frozen over puddle of water beside the road.

From the signs at the base of the tree, I came to the conclusion that a fisher had got caught in the trap and in a rare case, missed killing the animal outright. The fisher being a lot stronger that a marten, was able to straighten the nail and make its way to the open where he was possibly picked up by an eagle or hawk. I had a lynx caught in a marten set, a vertical box nailed to a tree. A timber wolf once stuck his paw into a mink set. The trap was anchored to a tree, but the wolf broke the chain.

I had acquired a hand gun, a twenty-two caliber magnum to dispatch live animals in traps, bears or wolves. The gun was purchased legally with an acquisition permit and registered with the RCMP in Ottawa. I applied for and received a permit to carry it on my trap line. I had to renew the permit every year with the Chief Firearms Officer in Toronto. Soon they started giving me a hard time. The first permit was valid for one year, after they changed it to September 1st to March 31st. The spring bear season was April 15th to June 15th, so I needed the gun during that period and I wasn't covered. Then one year after sending in my application for renewal, I received not a permit, but a letter stating that they were not issue any permits that year as they were conducting a study.

It so happened that was one of the times I caught a timber wolf in a snare by the body. He was alive in the snare. Being law abiding, I left the handgun locked in a safety box at home. I had no rifle with me, so the only option I had so he wouldn't suffer any longer was to dispatch him with a club. When I approached the wolf with the club, he knew what was coming, he just sat and howled. I felt so sorry for him, I would have given anything for those decision makers in Toronto to come and study this case.

The next year they did issue me a permit to carry the handgun, but with silly rules. The firearm must be worn on a belt on the outside of the clothing which is not feasible for a trapper being that we're in the mud, rain and snow. Then, the firearm must not be used for protection and they required a letter of proficiency signed by a Firearms Officer, stating I knew how to handle a gun. The harassment continued, they then wanted a letter from the Conservation Officer saying I needed the gun and that I traveled though swamps. Next they demanded I take a three day safety course, costing one hundred and sixty dollars, plus three days of my time and parking fees at the college. To top it all of I would have to repeat the course every years. That was the straw that broke my back, I sold the gun.

What did they accomplish? They can pat themselves on the back and say to the voters, "see we got another handgun off the streets". The fact is that the gun was only used for animals so they would not longer have to suffer and endure pain. In other words they only created hardship and inconvenience for me because I had to use methods to dispatch animals that I don't want to use. I tried carrying a rifle but it was a hindrance, with all the gear I have to haul around in a canoe and carry over portages a rifle is not an option. After the scope got banged I left the rifle at camp.

Some seasons I don't have to use a gun. A gun in a shoulder holster is not in the way and is there when I needed it. I would have like to have the gun in the holster when I checked a wolf snare and found a female wolf caught by her hind leg. I picked up a green club and approached the animal thinking when she gets to the end of the leash I would be able to hit her on the head. Instead, as I got close to her, she lunged at my face. I jerked back just in time as I felt her hot breath on my face. I didn't argue with her instead I went the ten miles back to camp a came back with the rifle. I would have liked to trade places with one of the decision makers in Toronto so he could feel the wolf's hot breath in his face.

There is a bear management unit which encompasses part of may trap line. The outfitter is entitled to a permit to carry a handgun for protection while bear baiting. On his permit is stamped, "For Protection Only". On my permit was stamped, "For Dispatching Live Animals in Traps Only, Not to be used for Protection".

Picture this scenario, the outfitter and I are walking down a trail on my trap line. We meet an aggressive bear. He can use his gun for protection, but I can't. Something is very wrong.

In June of 2007, I received a form in the mail that I had to fill out and return to renew the gun registration. After a month or so, I received a letter asking for additional information and phoned the telephone number provided. A female operator informed me vital information was missing. She said, "You are married to Verna", I answered, yes and have been for fifty-six years. She then asked me if I have lived with another woman in the past three years? I couldn't believe my ears, so I asked her to repeat the question. "Did you live with another woman in the past three years"? My response was, "No, certainly not, one woman is all I can handle". Then she says, "thank you that's all we needed to know. Your application will be processed in due time. Have a nice day" and hung up. So much for gun registration and gun control, it is law abiding gun owners that are bullied, harassed, regulated, legislated and ruled because it's easy, all the information is on file. Meanwhile gangs are able to easily acquire handguns to shoot each other with and an innocent bystander now and then.

The current Prime Minister of Canada, in his election campaign promised to scrap the gun registration if he was elected. He was elected and didn't get rid of the registration. Maybe that was another empty political promise, maybe he really meant it. When he got to the House, he found out he couldn't do what he wanted that easily. There was political horse trading. I'll let you milk my cow if you let me ride your horse and I'll also give you bonus of goat cheese. In the meantime, the gun registration is alive and unwell and the millions of tax payer dollars are f lowing into the sewer.

Two or three years ago there was an incident in Laval, Quebec, I believe where a police woman went to an apartment with a warrant. She knocked on the door and was answered with a fatal gun shot through the door. It turned out the shooter was a convicted felon barred from owning a firearm for ten years.

On a television news report, someone asked, "Why did the felon own two high powered rifles when he was barred from owning any firearms"? The reply, "because it was hunting season".

Perhaps if criminals were made to take a safety course, they would learn that guns are not used to shoot innocent bystanders or each other.

13

Animals seem to use the same trails year after year, that being, there are places where a trap or snare set produces animals every season. One such place was beside the trail into camp. The trail went past a Jack Pine tree about a foot in diameter. I thought rather than go around the tree with wire to anchor the snare; I would tie it to a dry pole about two inches thick and eight feet long, and then leaned it against the tree.

On the way to camp from home one day, driving the skidoo past the spot, I noticed that the pole was no longer there. I walked over, looked around but couldn't see any tracks where the pole could have been dragged. Then I noticed an unusual amount of loose bark at the base of the Jack Pine. I looked up the tree and about thirty feet was a dead lynx hanging over a branch on one side and the pole on the other side. The snare had closed around his body rather than his neck. He was able to climb the tree with the pole still attached to the snare. The natural grown Jack Pine trees are bare of branches, except near the top.

I thought to myself, how I am going to get this lynx down from up there. If I cut the tree down, the tree would damage the hide when it fell. The only other way I could think of was to build a ladder. I continued on to camp and when I got there I started a fire to heat the cabin and returned back to the Jack Pine tree with a chain saw, nails, hammer and the pulley rope hoist.

I cut down two poles about thirty feet long and three inches at the butt. If I built the ladder first I would not be able to lift it to lean it up against the tree. So I started a little at a time. I nailed several rungs, then lifted and inched the beginning of the ladder up against the tree. When I couldn't lift and pull it myself anymore, is used the rope hoist, one end on the tree and the other on the bottom rung. I would lift the ladder with one hand and pull on the hoist with the other. Slowly, inch by inch, rung by rung, I had the ladder built and leaning against the tree. I started up the ladder, but since I'm not too fond of height, I couldn't make it to the top where the lynx was. So I waited until it started to get dark, went up as far as I could, cut the wire and brought the lynx down in one piece.

About seventy-five yards up the hill at the back of the camp there is a cubby that was there when I took over. That is where I left the carcasses and bones of the skinned animals. Since it was constructed with only two entrances, one from each end, it was an ideal place for traps. I had set two number four traps there for lynx.

One day in November, I didn't leave the camp. I was tired and had to catch up on the skinning. It was late in the afternoon when I decided to check the cubby. As I neared the cubby I could see the anchor poles were in place, but when I got there I could only see one trap, the other trap was missing. I stood there scratching my head, how did the trap disappear without the anchor pole. Looking closer, I saw the wire around the pole had been tightened neatly. What happened was that I forgot to pass the wire through the trap chain before tightening it.

There was some snow on the ground with some bare patches, but enough snow for me to be able to see where a lynx had gone with the trap on his paw. I returned to camp and picked up the twenty-two magnum rifle, donned a light jacket as it was fairly mild and started to follow the lynx tracks. He followed the trail for a bit then veered to the left into the bush. Tracking was slow due to spots that were not covered with snow. Soon I could tell that I was closing in as the tracks showed he had started running. Suddenly, I noticed movement in the pines and saw him sitting, looking at me. I dispatched him with a bullet in his head. Picking him up, I then began to retrace my tracks back to camp. When I reached the trail it had started to get dark.

As I got back to camp I realized how close to disaster I had been. I left camp that late in the day with no compass, no matches, no flashlight, no warm clothes and no brains. Had the lynx led me a half hour further into the bush, I would not have been able to find my way back in the dark. The Higher Power, once again taking care of a fool.

In 2005, after arriving at camp from home, I decided to check some lynx snares. Even though it was late in the afternoon I was anxious to check the sets because there is always a possibility of the wolves getting there first. It happened once when checking the snare set all I found was a closed snare and one long piece of lynx intestine. The snares I checked were all empty until I came to the last one and discovered the snare was gone, even the wire from the tree was gone, not broken, just undone. There were no human tracks around so how did the anchor wire come undone.

Light snow had fallen the day before but tracks were still visible. Dusk had fallen but with the aid of a flashlight I concluded that a lynx was involved. There was little I could do in the dark, so I would come back the next day.

The next morning on the way to the snare set, I saw a marten cross the road in front of me. Following him into the bush I spotted him high up in a tree. I fired several shots but missed and he quickly disappeared.

When I arrived at the snare set I started looking for a sign. I saw signs of struggle and lynx tracks leading away. I followed the tracks and soon came to a round bare spot in the snow and then lynx tracks loping away. That told me the animal was injured and had lain at the same spot for a time long enough to melt the snow. Shortly after I spotted him standing in a clump of pines, I fired the gun; he stiffened his legs, stood for several seconds and began to lope away. That was my last bullet.

I had no idea whether I hit him or not. There was no use following him anymore since I had no more shells with me, besides if he wasn't followed he would probably lay down. After returning from camp with more ammunition I started to follow the tracks from where I left off. Following his tracks, I found him laying down a short distance from where he had been shot. Had I followed him after I first shot him, I might have saved myself a trip to camp and back for more shells. On the other hand he might have done what most animals generally do, keep going.

Upon checking the lynx I found the snare had close around his body by his hind quarters, the anchor wire was still attached to the snare. I came to the conclusion that when I twisted the wire tight around the tree, I left a tail end sticking out. In the struggle the wire kept going over the tail end until it came undone. Another lesson learned, always cut the excess wire off. Another thing worth writing about is that I have seen evidence of tracks in the snow where a lynx went through a loop six inches in diameter without disturbing the snare.

On the way to Wolf Lake, there is a productive snare set location in the brush beside a small lake at the edge of a stand of re-planted Jack Pine trees. After twenty years of growing the trees stand about ten feet tall.

I had set two snares for lynx; one was tied to a dry Jack Pine tree about three inches at the butt. There was no true handy way to anchor the other snare, so I wired it to a dry pole two inches by six feet long and leaned it against the brush. Arriving at the site I noticed the pole was gone. There were no signs of a struggle and no broken brush. The snare that was tied to the tree about ten feet away was lying on the ground. There were a couple inches of fresh snow and since there were no human tracks I assumed that the lynx got caught and took off with the pole. After looking around for some time I gave up.

A week later I returned to the site but in the meantime it had gotten mild and some of the snow melted. Checking the area carefully I pieced together what had occurred. I saw the snare on the ground and it was pulled apart. Picking up the snare and looking at it more closely I found the ferrule near the lock had come off. It was a snare that I had made and apparently didn't squeeze the ferrule tight enough. When the lynx felt the snare and the leaning pole settle around him, he instinctively lunged forward dragging the pole into the other snare. The sudden jerk caused the ferrule to slide off and the snare to come apart.

Through years of watching signs of animals, I learned some of their habits. At the first sign of danger, a lynx will head straight for thick bush so I began to search in the direction he would take and sure enough, not too far away I found him, lying dead, tangled in the brush. Incidentally, the dry Jack Pine tree the snare that had come apart was tied to is now a stump.

In November 2006, when I checked the sets I discovered the snare and the tree were gone. The missing snare caper was easy to solve. A moose had come along and stuck his leg in the snare, one yank and the tree became a stump. The moose is an inquisitive animal. Time and time again I noticed where they followed my tracks to the set and snoop around.

I can recall an incident early in my trapping career, when I set some three hundred and thirty traps through the ice at a beaver house. After setting the traps I filled the holes in the ice with snow so that the holes don't freeze too much, making it easier to open when I came back to check the traps. When I went back to check the traps, I saw tracks where a moose had followed my tracks to the beaver house and while snooping around stepped into the open hole covered with snow.

Lynx are also inquisitive animals and in learning their habits, they will always follow my footsteps when I walk off the trail to make a set for mink or marten. Now I don't make sets that are visible from the trail.

When I walk in the bush I pay attention and look for a good place for a snare, either between two trees or between two rocks. On the way back I set the snares. I've had good success with this system.

One time I made a lynx set along the trail. I hung a piece of beaver meat between two trees then placed branches and brush on either side, making an opening on each end. I placed two traps near the bait. The next morning when I came back to check the traps I had two lynx, one in each trap.

Regardless of how careful I try to be I still make mistakes. I had made a snare set for lynx, wiring the snare to a small tag alder. On checking the set after a fresh snowfall, I saw that the snare was gone, with no signs of struggle or broken brush. When I looked closer, I saw lynx tracks walking to the snare, the four paw prints close together about six feet on the other side. There was a hole in the snow where the anchor tag alder had been. I followed the tracks and soon found him tangled in the brush, dead. The tag alder the snare was tied to was also there. I then had seen that the small tree was dry and rotten at the base. Due to its instinctive forward lunging by the lynx and the sudden jerk dislodged the tree from it base. It was fortunate there was no snowfall to cover the tracks; otherwise the lynx would have been lost. Again I was reminded of the importance of proper anchoring of snares and traps.

14

I try to harvest all the beaver in open water as there is a lot less work involved than trapping under ice.

Leg hold traps are allowed for drowning sets. The trap is set near shore just below surface. It is placed so that the beaver will step into it as he emerges from the water. A length of fourteen gauge wire is tied to a rock which is then thrown into the water deep enough to keep the beaver submerged. The wire is pulled taut and tied to a stake driven into the ground near the trap. The chain of the trap is attached to a slide lock on the wire. When the beaver gets caught, he instinctively dives into deep water. The slide lock prevents the beaver from surfacing. When the stored oxygen is used up the beaver dies painlessly.

Generally a 330 conibear trap is used. It measures ten and a half inches square and has a powerful spring on each side. When a beaver enters the trap it touches the trigger and both bars at the top and bottom slam on the animal, killing or rendering it unconscious almost instantly. The trap must be placed where the beaver would most likely enter it. Beavers dragging branches for their winter food cache enter the water at the same place, which is known as a run. That is an ideal location for a set, providing the water is deep enough to submerge at least half of the trap. Some runs cannot be set if the water is too shallow and the bottom is rocky. Two stakes are driven into the ground in the water and the trap placed so that the trigger is submerged. Some sets require branches placed so as to direct the beaver into the trap.

Another type of set is a diving set. The 330 trap is suspended on a dry pole, (the beaver would chew a green one) about two inches in diameter. The pole is then placed on the surface of the water. When the beaver swims up to the pole he will dive under the pole rather than go over top and into the trap.

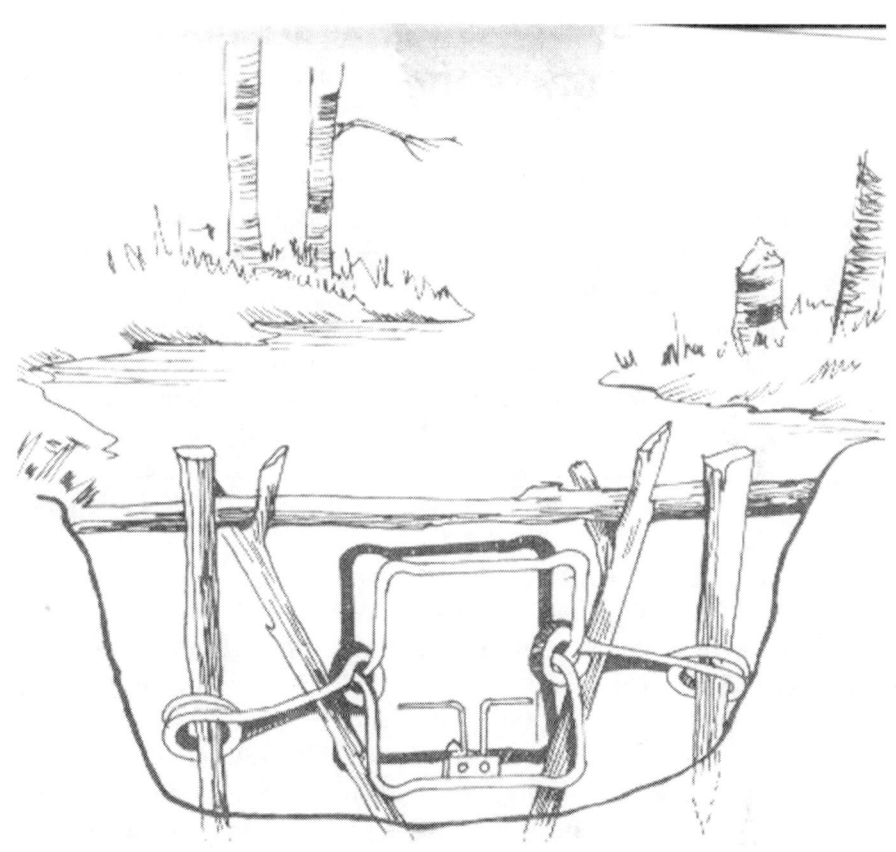

Then there is the lure set. Lure bait is made mainly from beaver castors. A trap is position in the water in a place where a beaver would swim into it rather than around it and then some bait is placed behind the trap. These sets are placed well away from the house. Since beaver are very territorial, a strange beaver scent will bring the beaver into the trap. Some houses have paths where beavers climb to the top to plaster the house with mud. If the conditions are favorable, traps could be placed at such runs.

Occasionally a trap can be set at the entrance to the house in open water. There were times when I spotted the entrance from the canoe; an entrance is a tunnel at the bottom leading up into the house. A 330 conibear trap can be anchored vertically on a dry pole and then lowered into the water so that the trap faces the entrance. The pole must be secured to stay upright and believe me that is not always possible. A beaver entering or exiting the house will enter the trap.

Green poplar works well as bait. A poplar pole with a little bark peeled off is placed in an upright position on shore near the water and then a trap is placed where the beaver will travel to get the bait. At some sets, dry branches maybe used to guide the beaver into the trap.

No two houses are the same. Some are easy to set, providing conditions are favorable, the runs are good, the water is an ideal depth and the ground good enough for driving the stakes in. Some are difficult to set due to no visible runs and the water being too shallow and rocky bottom. The main objective is to set a trap where a beaver would most likely enter it. That comes with experience. I'm still learning and continue making errors in anchoring the traps.

One time I went to the west end of Schist Lake to check a beaver set. When I arrived I saw the trap was missing. Considering the location, I was fairly certain no human had taken it. Had it been at the start of my trapping career I would have given up, now I thought there was a good chance it was at the bottom of the lake.

I went back to camp and returned with a garden rake to drag the bottom for the trap. The water was too deep, so I tied a slender pole for an extension. After many attempts, I was able to hook and pull the trap up with the beaver in it to surface. I checked the chain on the trap and there was no wire on it, so it was clear that I had forgotten to tie the trap to an anchor pole.

A similar incident happened on Yeo Lake, on the creek where I dragged the canoe the first year. When I had got there to check the set, I saw the trap was gone and one stake was missing. My first thought was that some moose hunters had lifted it, however the odds were the trap was on the bottom. Again using the rake I was successful in bringing the trap and beaver to the surface. Occasionally a beaver is eaten by a lynx, fox, wolf or bear before they hibernate. Once again, it is important that the traps are checked often.

In 1984, Eddie Forest Company was harvesting logs in the area. They complained to the Ministry of Natural Resources that beaver had flooded the road in two places. One dam was on my trap line and the other on the adjacent trap line belonging to another trapper. Since that trapper lived in the Toronto area I was authorized to trap both locations. The Ministry supplied me with live traps and I was able to relocate the beavers to other lakes. The live traps were made from heavy wire mesh and were shaped like a large oyster shell with both halves opening flat when the trap was set. When the beaver tripped the trigger, a powerful spring closed the trap with the beaver inside and unharmed.

Trapping beaver through ice requires more work and effort. A live house is more difficult to locate as all is snow covered.

A house must be approached very carefully. Over the entrance, with all the activity of the beaver the ice is very thin; therefore the ice must be checked with an ice chisel before walking on it. A hole is then made in the ice so the entrance of the house can be located. Usually the tunnel is under the food cache, so all the branches must be removed. I use a hockey stick with an extension bolted and use the blade to locate the tunnel. When it is located I make sure there is no debris to prevent the trap from working properly. Then I wire the trap to a dry pole and lower the pole into the water so the trap faces the tunnel. I lay a pole horizontally against the upright pole and wire them together. The water in the hole will soon freeze and hold the upright pole in position.

Another type of set that could be used under the ice is a bait set. Again, a 330 conibear trap is wired to a dry pole with the trigger wires bent horizontally with a slender green poplar stick wired to the trigger. Lowering the pole into the water in an upright position, the trap should be positioned half way between the bottom and the ice. A horizontal pole holds the upright pole in place until the water freezes.

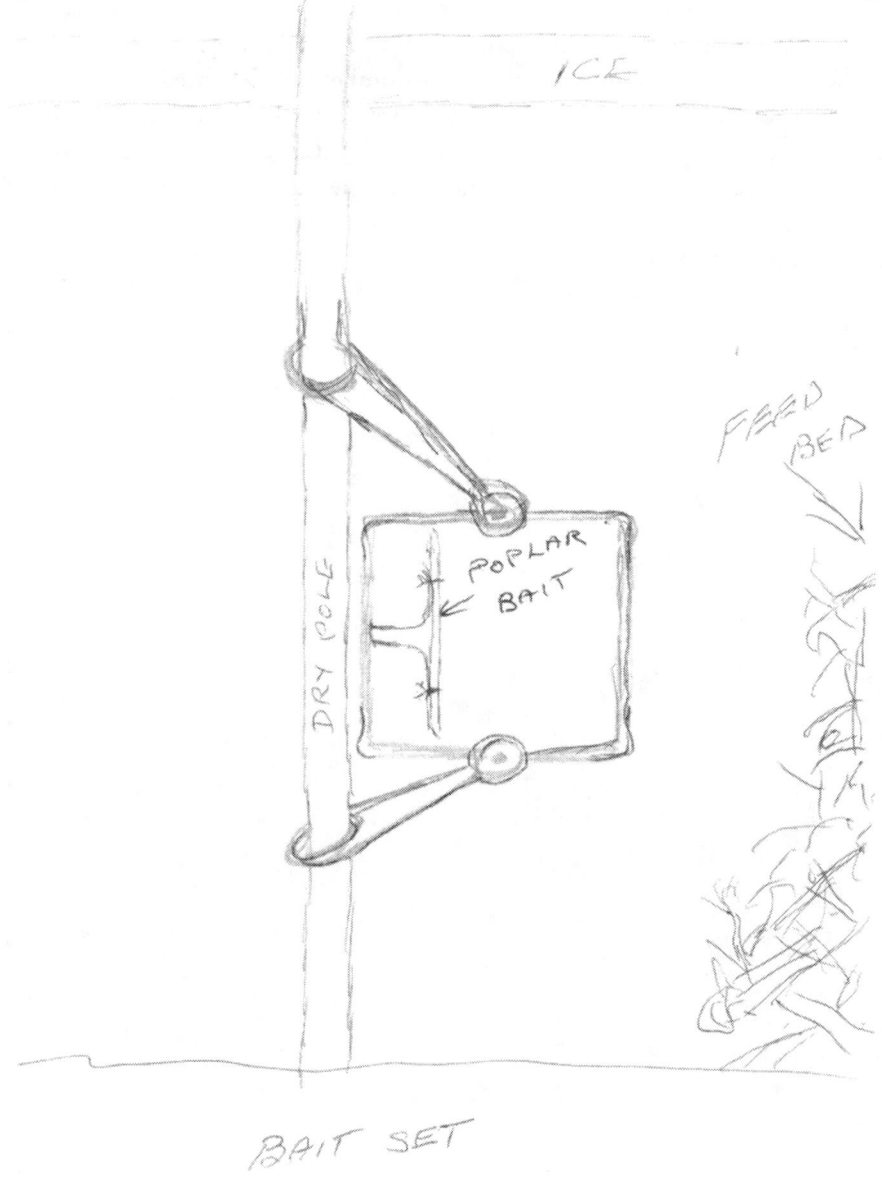

A snare set is effective particularly in late winter when the food pile becomes stale, fresh poplar is very enticing. A green poplar pole about two inches thick and long enough to extend above the ice from the bottom of the pond. A fourteen gauge wire is fastened along the pole from one end to the other. Without the wire, the snares would be lost as beaver would chew the pole into pieces. Two snares with an eight inch loop are then wired to the pole, one on each side with another two wired above the first two. The number of snares used depends on the depth of the water. A hole is then cut in the ice near the food pile large enough to accommodate the pole with the snares. Water must be checked for branches that would stop the snares from closing. The snare pole is lowered and held upright by a horizontal pole beside it. Multiple catches are common. I have pulled out four beaver on one snare pole.

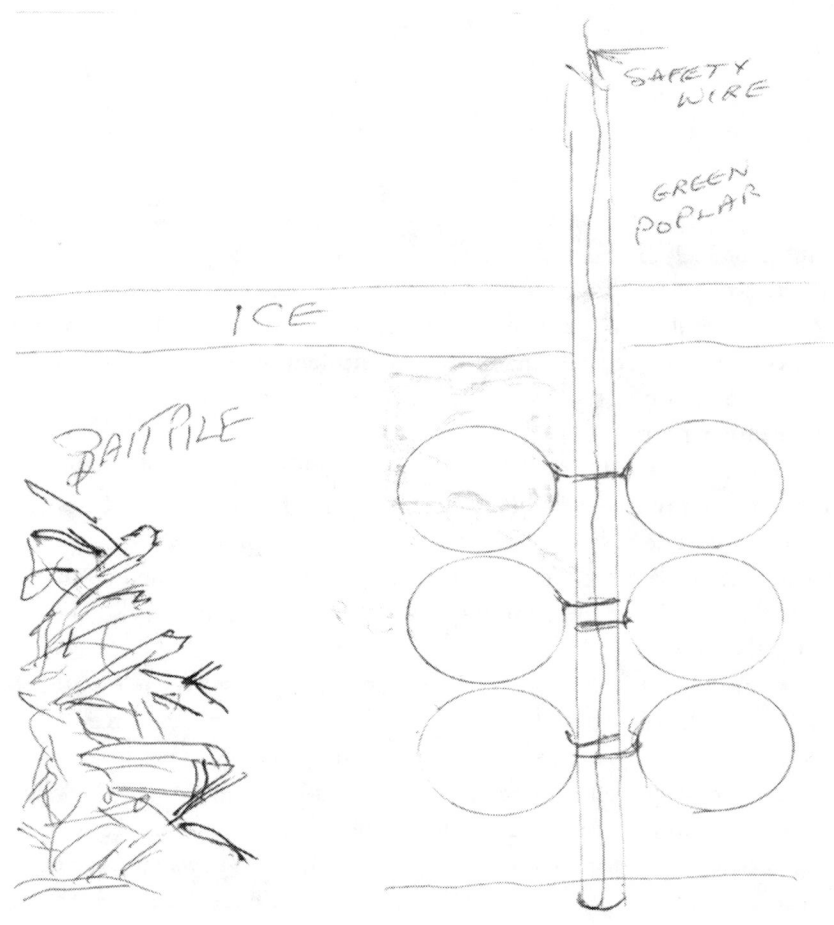

15

In September of 1994, I had a setback.

In August we visited our eldest daughter, Linda in Sarnia. I wasn't feeling good, nothing I could really put my finger on, no pain, just tired, no ambition. Linda works at a clinic and she made an appointment for me to see a physician there. I got a number of tests; x-rays, EKG, blood tests and all results came back showing nothing wrong.

In September at camp, I bent down to pick something up and felt a sharp pain on the right side of my chest. I thought nothing of it; after all I just had a physical a few weeks prior. The first week in October while trapping bear, one snare set had a closed empty snare every morning when I checked it. I decided I would try to shoot the bear, so I put the climbing tree stand on the tree ready to climb up and wait for the bear.

The next morning I was up early, it was still dark outside. I felt awful so I didn't eat any breakfast. I started out on the *ATV* when I came to a tree that had fallen across the trail. I took the chain saw and prepared to cut the tree off the trail. As I bent down I felt another sharp pain which I also ignored. When I reached the truck and started loading the supplies I'd need I was really feeling sick. I began to sweat and my chest felt as if a bear had his paws around me and was squeezing me. The pain didn't last long but I continued feeling awful. Still not thinking anything was seriously was wrong I kept on going.

Once arriving at the tree stand I prepared to climb up. The stand consists of two pieces, one for the feet and the other to sit on. Each is anchored to the tree by a flat bar on each side of the tree. I put my weight on my arms; lift the bottom with my feet before anchoring and so climb, repeating the sequence. There should have been a safety rope attached to the bottom part just in case the stirrup slipped off my feet and fell.

When I started to climb I realized I had forgotten the safety rope. I took a chance hoping the bottom wouldn't slip off my feet. When I was about six feet above the ground, sure enough the bottom slipped off my feet and fell to the ground. Somehow I managed to scramble to the ground. Still not feeling well I decided to pack it in for the day.

Returning to camp, I then went to lie down on the cot and soon fell asleep. I woke up at 10:30 am feeling a little better. I hadn't have any chest pains since the tightening pressure on my chest earlier in the morning,

I debated with myself should I try for the bear again the next morning or do I go home and seek medical attention. Common sense won, I packed up and headed home.

In the crossroad on the way out, I came upon two Ministry of Natural Resource trucks, with the canine unit and several Conservation Officers. Getting out of the truck to see what was going on; they told me they were after a culprit that had poached a cow moose. I then mentioned to them that I wasn't feeling well and told them of the pain that I had experienced. The CO for my area offered to drive my truck to Highway 144, but I declined because I was feeling fairly good and I would have to drive the rest of the way to Sudbury anyways.

I arrived home at 3:30 pm, had a shower, ate a sandwich because I didn't eat anything for breakfast and then headed to a walk in clinic. When I got to the clinic the doors were locked and a sign stating that the hours were from 7 pm to 9 pm, so I went back home and waited until seven. When I returned at seven to the clinic and told the doctor what had occurred, he told me I was in the wrong place and that I belonged at the hospital Emergency Room. He asked me which hospital I preferred so that he could phone ahead and tell them to expect me and there would be no waiting time.

I left the clinic and went home and had Verna drive me to the hospital not knowing if they would keep me over night or not. Getting to the hospital I enter the E.R., they were waiting for me and I was immediately laid on a gurney and quickly attached wires connected to a heart monitor and blood samples were taken. Shortly after being monitored and the blood sample results came back, the doctor gave me the good news, I did not suffer a heart attack but they were going to keep overnight for observation. Overnight stretched into two weeks and during that time I had a stress test on a treadmill and it was then determined that I have a blocked artery, but they didn't know where or how bad.

I was put on medication, told to take it easy and make an appointment with a cardiologist and was finally discharged. Once at home I called the cardiologist to book the appointment and to my amazement, the earliest date they had available was in the first week of January, almost three months away.

Trapping season opened while I was still in the hospital therefore getting a late start. Joe, a trapper buddy of mine from Gogama was able to assist me with my trapping and we managed to fill my quota. Also the Gods were smiling down at me with a late freeze up that year. We were still using the canoe in open water on November 15th.

The ordeal I had experience had taken its toll on me. I began to have panic attacks, depression and was full of fear at times. I had to force myself to go to camp and do things I loved to do before. I did not experience anymore chest pains. I should mention that Verna was diagnosed with angina some time before I had my problems. She had chest pains and used nitro glycerin spray to alleviate the pain.

I soon learned the importance of a proper diet. Thinking my diet was fine always eating whole wheat bread, pancakes made with whole wheat flour and besides that I didn't drink or smoke for years and by no means was I overweight. But I use to buy restaurant bacon by the case and used hydrogenated margarine by the case. Breakfast at camp usually was pancakes smeared with margarine, six slices of bacon and an egg in the pancake batter. The next morning was six slices of bacon, four slices of whole wheat bread loaded with hydrogenated margarine and two eggs. Next day pancakes again. Often I would fry a pan full of side pork and eat it all with boiled potatoes and dill pickles.

After some research I educated myself about good fat and bad fats, hydrogenated oil and processed foods. With that new found knowledge I changed our diet completely. Along with taking our prescribed medication, Verna and I started taking vitamins and supplements.

In January we both went to see the cardiologist. After checking us over the doctor had prescribed us additional medication and told Verna to come back in six months. Then addressing me he said, "You're trucking all alone on your trap line, I'm going to send you for a dye test to see where that blocked artery is and just how blocked it is.

The test was scheduled for early February 1995. There were four of us, an overweight woman, two other men and me. After performing the test he said to the woman that she had to go home lose some weight and to come back in a year. The other two men needed bypass surgery and he then informed me that I had one artery that was ninety percent blocked and two arteries that were each blocked ten percent. The two arteries that were blocked ten percent were really not an issue but the one artery blocked ninety percent we'll try inserting a balloon, which is know as angioplasty. The procedure was performed at the Memorial Hospital in Sudbury the first week in April and all went well.

Verna and I were both scheduled for an annual checkup. Amazingly, Verna's pains stopped and she didn't have to use the glycerin spray anymore and the prescribed glycerin for me, I had no occasion to use it.

In June of 1995, I started clearing the trails of brush that I had neglected for the last few years. Before where I had no energy or ambition to do anything, I was now able to work with zest and enthusiasm. The trails were so over grown that in places I had to kneel down and look close to the ground to see where the trail was.

By the end of September using the brush cutter and a chain saw I had cleared a total of thirteen miles of trails much to the delight of hunters. There was so much *ATV* traffic that the trails are still passable today.

In the fall during moose season, while driving my *ATV* down the road, I came to a couple camped beside their truck. They waved me down and started talking excitedly. It seemed that we met five years ago during their hunt and after meeting me then they often wondered if I was still around and how I was doing. The couple was in their eighties and from Parry Sound. During our conversation the lady said that a lot of people asked her if she worried about dying at her age. She told them, "heck no, I know the time will come some day, but I don't dwell on it. I feel fine and live each day to the fullest". Whether it was what she said or how she said it, I felt a great improvement in my depression. In the forest, like Willie Nelson, I finally found an ace that I could keep.

Our yearly checkup went well. After her second checkup with the cardiologist, he had told Verna that she had no need to come back anymore. He said that she was fine and that she probably did not have angina, just stomach pains. Her condition had reversed itself. A year later he told me not to come back anymore because I was well.

To this day we still follow our low fat diet and take herbal supplements. I do not recommend or condemn taking them but it what works for us.

When moving to Timmins in 1997, our new family doctor we found took Verna and me off our prescribed heart medication saying we both were fine.

16

I am a former smoker. I used to love the smell and taste of tobacco smoke. My dad used to try to discourage me from smoking, but I couldn't wait till I left home so that I could smoke without being harassed.

At that time the harmful effects of smoking were not as well known as they are today. Even doctors were used in cigarette ads.

Smoking did not cause any problems in my like. I tried to quit several times without success. In the mid seventies there was an aid to quit smoking on the market. It consisted of four cigarette holders. It was recommended to use number 1 for two weeks, which eliminated fifty-five percent of the nicotine, number 2 for two weeks eliminating sixty-five percent of nicotine, number 3 for two weeks, this one eliminating seventy-five percent of nicotine and then the number 4 cigarette holder for two weeks eliminating ninety percent. During that time the body would get accustom to less nicotine gradually and make it easier to quit.

My hunting buddy Leo was using it also trying to quit smoking and told me that it did work. Although I really didn't try to quit in the year and a half I used it, but I did feel better in my chest. Every second day I pulled the holder apart to clean it and I would look at that black stinky syrup, being the nicotine and thought to myself, that if it wouldn't be for that holder all that nicotine would be in my lungs. My brain just couldn't seem to accept the fact and I continued smoking.

In January 1977, Leo spent sometime in Florida on a holiday. While there he ran short of Canadian cigarettes and didn't like the taste of the American cigarettes and that is where and how he quit smoking.

In July, Leo had his travel trailer parked at a lake on Manitoulin Island. One weekend he invited us to go fishing. On the way there I bought a carton of Players cigarettes paying seven dollars and fifty cent. While fishing Leo told me about his quitting and said to me, "you'd better quit smoking or else I'll throw you're cigarettes away when we go moose hunting in the fall". I told him that I would give it an honest try after I finished the carton I had just bought on the way there.

It was a Sunday evening when I finished the last package of the carton of cigarettes. Waking Monday morning I told myself that I would try not smoking today. I was driving taxi cab part time in those days and I have to admit the first day was hard. The desire was not that strong because of using the number four cigarette holder I used all the time but the habit was every few minutes my hand would automatically go to my shirt pocket for the cigarette pack. I said to myself, "I'll buy just one more pack and then I'll quit" but instead I held on one hour at a time and before you know it the day was done and I did not buy that pack of cigarettes.

The second day was a little easier. After the third day I had no desire for a cigarette and the habit was gone. I was able to have a coffee without a cigarette and I didn't have to have a cigarette after a meal. It was as if I never smoked in my life. There was a complete turn around from loving to hating cigarettes. I cannot stand the smell of tobacco smoke which at one time I loved so much. I even have to leave an area if there is someone smoking nearby.

Several people have said to me that I have strong self control. Not so, if I want a cigarette badly and I don't light one, that's self control. But I have no desire for one so self control does not apply. Talking with a lot of people, they tell me that they still have the desire to smoke even after years of quitting.

It is a known fact that tobacco addiction is very difficult and in some cases impossible to over come. Why was I successful? If I had any doubts about my Higher Power, this was proof beyond the shadow of a doubt that He is with me. The sad thing about this happening is that Leo, who was such a strong influence in my quitting smoking, is no longer with us. Apparently he waited too long to quit and developed lung cancer in the early 1990's and died shortly after. It could be argued that the Higher Power had nothing to do with my quitting smoking and it would have happened anyhow.

This brings to mind a fable my Dad told me when I was a boy. In Ukraine, in the late 1880's, there lived a peasant with his wife. He was fortunate enough to own a horse, unlike everyone else who lived in poverty. One day his wife got seriously ill and the peasant got scared. He said to God, "If you make my wife well, I'll sell my horse and donate the money to the church". Soon his wife was well and the peasant loathe to part from his horse saying to himself, "aw, she would have gotten well anyway", so he kept the horse.

The next week his wife got sick again. This time she was sicker than before. The peasant once more turned to God. "I know I'm at fault for not keeping my promise I made before, but if You save my wife, I swear I'll sell my horse and donate the money to the church". Amazingly the wife soon got well and she was her old, cheerful self again. The peasant was afraid to go back on his promise, so he took his horse and cat to the market. A buyer checked out the horse, liking it he ask the peasant the price. "One ruble', said the peasant. The buyer not believing his ears gave the peasant one ruble for the horse. The peasant told the buyer that he could not sell the horse without the cat. The buyer then asked the peasant how much he wanted for the cat. "One hundred rubles for the cat", the peasant replied. The buyer thought that was a fair price and paid one hundred rubles, took the cat and lead the horse away.

And so the peasant kept his promise to God and sold his horse and donated the one ruble to the church that he got for the horse. There is no record of what became of the peasant or his wife.

17

In the fall of 1983, I was fortunate to draw a cow tag. We now have a lottery for moose; you just can't go out and shoot what you see. I had my 308 gun in the boot of the *ATV*, while on my run checking traps.

One late afternoon I was driving on Chester Road back to camp, when I came to a small side road that continued for a short distance then looped back to Chester Road. I had been on this road before and saw a lot of fresh moose tracks. On an impulse I turned left onto the road. As I topped a little knoll, I saw two moose standing in a cut over about a hundred yards in the distance. I looked at the moose and didn't see any horns, so I was okay to shot. I inserted the clip, aimed at the closest one and fired. It went down. When I walked over I saw small knobs where the horns are suppose to be, which meant I had bagged a male calf.

I field dressed him, affixed my tag and left the moose there. The next morning I went back towing a trailer. I was able to drag the moose out with the *ATV* and load it on the trailer.

In 1985, I was awarded a Bull Moose tag in the draw. I scouted the area around Rat and Squawman Lakes. There were a few cutovers with access roads. I found lots of moose signs again.

One morning while I was driving my *ATV* on a small access road when the road became too rough to continue, so I hopped off and started to walk. Suddenly there was a moose ahead of me. I checked but it was the wrong model, it was a cow and I had a bull tag so I couldn't shoot it. So I stood there and watch it walk away.

The next morning it was raining, but stopped before noon, so I had a late start. I returned to the same area, parked at the same promising spot with open areas and starting moose calling. However, due to the lack of patience I moved to another spot and started calling again. I should have learned about patience, but I didn't.

In the late 1970's, I was hunting moose alone in the Ignace area. I drove the cutover bush roads and camped in my van. One morning I drove into an access road which branched off the main road. It ended a short distance later. There was good visibility in all directions and a lot of moose tracks. I thought that would be a good place to camp for a day or two. However, due to lack of patience again, I soon moved thinking I'd see a moose over the next hill.

I drove to the main road, turned left and parked on a hill a short distance away. About fifteen minutes later I watched a pick up truck driving on the road then turn into the road I had just came out from. A few minutes later I heard a shot, driving to the spot where I left I saw the hunters had bagged a big bull moose. Patience would have been rewarded that morning.

I drove up the road where I had seen the cow moose. After a short distance I looked up and saw a bull moose standing broadside on a hill about three hundred and fifty yards away. I checked with the scope to make sure he wore a rack of horns. I tried to get a little closer, but when I saw him getting nervous I decided to shoot. I aimed and fired. He still stood there, I fired another shot and he turned around facing the other direction. I fired two more shots and watched him move from sight.

I inserted a fresh clip in the gun and walked to where I though the moose was standing when I shot him. Looking around I didn't see anything, then I looked back and couldn't see the *ATV*, so when I moved over to where I could see the *ATV* and checked around I noticed the horns sticking out from the brush. I walked up to him and saw that I had gotten a large moose with a big rack of antlers. I field dressed him, affixed my tag and went back to camp. There I collected all the equipment I needed hooked up the trailer and drove to the kill site.

I made the road passable so that the *ATV* could be driven up to the moose, I tried to pull the moose with the *ATV* but it wouldn't budge. I cut it in half, tried again with still no success. I cut it into quarters and I was not able to lift a quarter. I left the hide on and dragged them one at a time to the truck. The trailer had a winch in front so I managed to drag them onto the trailer using the loading ramp. I pushed them into the truck.

I made five trips from the kill site to the truck. The fifth trip was to haul out the head with the antlers. By the time I finished I ran out of daylight and energy. I couldn't push the head in far enough to close the tailgate.

It was ten pm when I passed a moose hunter's camp beside the road. There was a light on so I stopped and asked for assistance. With their help we got the tailgate closed and I was on the way home to Sudbury.

A few days, later I went an outfitters fly in camp in the Chapleau area. The head with the antlers was still in the back of the truck. A plane was landing bringing back a party of American moose hunters from their hunting trip and sadly returning empty handed. When they saw the antlers one of them asked me if I wanted to sell them and if so what did I wanted for them. "What are they worth to you" I asked. "How about a hundred dollars", the American said. "You got 'em", I said. After we removed the antlers, he then said, "Boy I wish I had the bullet that killed this moose". As it happened while dressing the animal I came upon the bullet, removed it and put it in my coat pocket. After returning home I didn't empty my pockets, so his wish was fulfilled and I handed him the bullet. Somewhere in Tennessee, U.S., over someone's mantle still hang the antlers.

18

During my early years on the trap line, many incidents were due to my inexperience. Fortunately none ended in disaster.

When I bought my first chain saw, a twelve inch McCollaugh, I didn't even know it had an oil tank for the chain. There came a time when it wouldn't make a straight cut. I would cut a tree and it would be on a curve instead of up and down. Thinking there was something wrong with it, I brought it back to the dealer. He explained to me that the chain was sharpened more on one side than the other. It seems one side is easier to sharpen and the other side more awkward.

At one time while on a run checking traps, a clanging noise developed in the front of the snow machine. I opened the cover, but couldn't see the source of the noise. I turned around and returned to camp. I sure was glad to see two guys ice fishing in the bay close to the camp. I went to see them, telling them about the noise. After them checking we soon found the problem. It seemed the bolt in the clutch had come loose. They were able to repair the clutch. Had I not returned to camp the bolt would have fallen out and the clutch would have come apart. I just didn't know all the bolts should be checked occasionally.

One time while trapping beaver through the ice, I made a snare set near a beaver house. After lowering the pole with the snares, I wired a horizontal pole to keep it upright. Thinking the water would freeze and anchor the pole I didn't tighten the wire too tight. It got mild and the water did not freeze like I thought it would. When a large beaver got caught in a snare, he managed to pull the snare pole through the wire. One of the lessons I learned early, is that when in danger, the beaver heads for the safety of the house. In this case the pole prevented him from entering the house and there he remained. When his stored oxygen ran out he painlessly died. I had to tie a hook to a pole and locate the entrance. I was able to find it and hooked the pole and retrieved the beaver.

Another episode I just recalled. One fall, there was snow on the ground with some bare patches. I was brushing out a trail, glad it was cold enough to keep the snakes away. Imagine to my surprise when I saw a snake slithering over a patch of snow. I dropped the brush cutter and ran for the twelve gauge shot gun I had on the *ATV* and when I looked around I saw the snake draped over a log. One shot blew it away.

I'm happy to say my fright of snakes is lessening. Two years ago, Verna and I killed two with a stick. Verna was outside with a broom when I heard her call, "Vic". I answered, "Where it is", knowing she was yelling about a snake. "Should I bring the gun" I hollered. "No, I have it pinned down", she said. I went out and killed it with a stick and tossed it away.

I had cut slabs of wood out of a big tree and made steps going up to the cabin from the dock. One day on the way to the cabin from fishing, Verna was ahead of me. When she got to the top of the stairs she saw a snake and pinned it with her walking stick. That one I also killed and tossed away. What a difference from the time while building the shed.

Through the years I upgraded the *ATV* from a Honda Big Red three wheeler to a 500 Arctic Cat 4x4, with a winch and hand warmers. In the early 1990's, while trading up an *ATV* at Sudbury Boat and Canoe, the owner, Gary, expressed an interest in trapping. I invited him to come to camp with me some weekend. He came and liked it so much he kept coming back. Eventually he took the trapping course and obtained this 02 trappers license, which is a helper. He has been my helper for years; in fact he will take over the trap line when I am no longer able to be active.

I had often worried through the years of what I would do with cabin and equipment if the succeeding trapper did not wish to purchase them. The law is that if the incoming trapper does not buy it, I must then remove the cabin or let him have it for nothing. I owned the cabin and contents but not the land and the cabin can only be used by the licensed trapper.

This is only one example of the many "what if" thoughts. Like crossing the bridge before it's built. I still have negative thoughts on occasions. I know what to do, but I don't know how to do it. I try to be more positive.

On October 19th, 2003, I checked a 330 conibear trap set in water on Schist Lake. Nearing the trap I could see it was closed with something in it. Imagine to my surprise when I pulled it out of the water and saw a mink and a rabbit in the trap side by side.

A mink in the water is normal, but a rabbit is a land animal and does not go into water. My theory is that the mink was chasing the rabbit, which out of desperation jumped into the water, just as the mink got alongside and tried to grab the rabbit by the throat and hitting the trigger and the 330 slammed shut. A multiple catch in a conibear is nothing unusual, but a rabbit and mink are. I believe it's a one and only possibly, one for the Guinness Book of Records. I didn't have a camera with me but there were some hunters camped near where I park my truck. I went over to see if they had a camera and one guy did. I borrowed the camera and was able to document the proof.

In early December of the same year, Gary was over for the weekend. We tried ice fishing about two hundred yards away from the camp. One time I paced off the distance because I shot an otter from the doorway of the camp early in the fall using a twenty-two magnum rifle with a scope. That's why I know the distance.

On Sunday afternoon Gary had lifted the fishing lines and prepared to leave for home. He loaded his equipment on the *ATV* and left for the truck. I was about ready to follow when I looked out the window and saw at the fishing site what looked like the ice chisel standing upright with a jacket handing from it. As I liked closer and wondered if Gary had forgotten something, I saw it move. I then realized I was looking at a timber wolf. My first impulse was to reach for the twenty-two magnum rifle, which was encased under my bunk. Then I remembered that the 308 rifle was on the *ATV* ready to take out to the truck. The door of the camp faces the lake, so the wolf saw me as I went for the gun.

I returned with the gun and in the excitement I couldn't find the clip so, I just inserted one cartridge into the breech. In the meantime the wolf had slowly trotted about three hundred and fifty yards into the distance. I aimed and fired. His hind quarters went down and he spun around several times, then he stood up and slowly trotted away into the bush. I walked out to where the wolf had stood when I shot him and there was lot of urine on the snow and urine leaking to the side of his tracks. Apparently I hit him in his bladder. I followed the tracks and soon there was blood, but not enough to be fatal. He led me through the densest bush there was. I soon gave up reasoning that if left alone he would lie down and stiffen up. I went pack to the cabin and didn't go home.

The next morning I took up the tracking where I had left off. There was no sign of where he had laid down or was getting weak. I gave up; there was no chance I would ever catch up to him. I came out of the bush on to the lake, quite a distance past the spot where the wolf had stood. It was a sunny day, and I looked ahead I noticed a long thin straight furrow in the snow, then smooth, another shorter furrow, then smooth snow, then a short sort of dotted furrow and at the end of which lay the spent bullet.

The bullet had gone through the wolf and continued until it gradually lost its velocity and dropped in the snow. What are the odds of this ever happening? I still have the bullet.

In September of 2005, Gary and I were out in search on live beaver houses. We paddled across Chain Lake and portaged into Attach Lake. We were not far from shore as beaver houses are mostly found near shore, when Gary spotted something that looked like the tip of moose antlers. We went closer and checked it out and sure enough there was a bull moose lying at the base of a sheer cliff with his head resting against the rock. He appeared to be about four years old with a nice rack of antlers.

We reported the discovery to the Conservation Officer and he said that he would be out to check it out. He was out the day after and I showed him the location where the moose was. There were no wounds visible and no blood, so we concluded that the moose for some reason or other fell of the cliff and broke his neck. It appeared to have happened very recently as there was no smell or flies. With the CO assisting us, we removed the antlers because Gary said that he would like to get them mounted. I passed by the carcass several weeks later and found it intact. There were no signs of ravens or wolves. As a rule ravens are first on the scene and by the time they are done they leave only the hide and the bones.

19

As I look at the past, I can see the dumb things I have done or things that I didn't do that could have easily turned into a disastrous situation, but didn't.

There is a fish camp on the east end of Schist Lake, built on an island. They keep one boat at the landing, about three quarters of a mile from the end of the road. When they come up fishing, all their gear has to be transported over the rough trail by and *ATV.*

One time a gang of eight from Delhi, which is located in Southern Ontario, came and arranged for me to have their supplies brought over by land. When they were ready to return home I hauled their gear out to their truck. I made four trips with a loaded trailer and a load on the front and the rear racks of the *ATV.* After unloading I returned the mile and a half to camp and as I was getting ready to roll the trailer into the garage, I noticed on wheel askew. When I shook the trailer, I found the wheel loose on the hub, two stud bots were missing and the other two were half out, but there was no damage. I got new stud bolts when I went home, repaired the wheel and all was well. Had I made one more trip the wheel would have fallen off and I would have been in serious trouble because I had no way of repairing the wheel.

In the late 1980's, I bought a twenty-five percent share in a licensed restaurant. I did everything wrong right from the start. I didn't check the financial statements of the business, I didn't have my own lawyer and I knew absolutely nothing about running a business. Given all that I should have lost my shirt, yet it turned out to be a profitable investment. There seems to be some Power that always makes wrong things right.

In May of 2006, Verna developed a white spot on her bottom lip. After checking the spot our family doctor referred her to a surgeon. The surgeon operated and a biopsy was done, the diagnosis was skin cancer. Due to the location he was not able to remove it all because it would have made the lip look too deformed, so referred her for radiation. There is no such service in Timmins, so he referred us to the Cancer Center in Sudbury.

The Cancer Center in Sudbury called us up and the earliest appointment they could get for Verna was in August. I didn't feel comfortable with the long waiting period and began checking other cities that had Cancer Centers. After calling a clinic in London with some success, I had the surgeon fax Verna's report to them. I waited until Monday to phone the clinic and to my astonishment they told me to bring her in on Thursday of that week. Dr. Gilchrest is one of the top oncologists there, but he is semi retired, yet we were fortunately enough that he was there to examine Verna. He suggested a new treatment as opposed to radiation which has to be administered every day for two weeks not to mention the unpleasant side effects. The procedure would take less that an hour, consisted of injecting radio active gold grains into her lip. The success rate was very high. The machine that produced the gold grains in Hamilton was down so we had to return to the clinic on June 22nd after they received the gold grains to get the injections done. One small draw back was that we had to keep a certain distance from her because the injections made her radio active. Not knowing this, my daughter had to drive Verna back to Sarnia in the back seat of the car, then drive back to London and pick me up. She couldn't sit at the dinner table with us, I was not allowed to sleep in the same bed for a week and even Tippy who loved Verna so much couldn't even sit at her feet or on her lap. At the September follow up appointment Dr. Gilchrest pronounced her cancer free, he also said the little bumps on the inside of her lip that she could feel were the gold grains in the skin and would remain there.

In May 2007, Verna complained of a swollen lip and lumps. I decided to take her for a check up in London to be on the safe side. I phoned the Cancer Clinic in London on Tuesday and they told me Dr. Gilcherst would see her in Sarnia on Friday. The nurses knew we have a daughter living in Sarnia so we didn't even have to drive to London. After the doctor checking Verna he said all was normal. Now I have a radio active wife. She was issued a card stating she's radio active as she'll fail any security check and set the alarms off.

The incident has little to do with trapping; I mention it only to point out the influence of the Higher Power in our daily lives. I contacted London and I did request that the surgeon to fax the report, but I had no control over the events that occurred afterwards. Dr. Gilchrest being there at the time, being semi retired, the appointment in three days, when the average waiting period is three month, and also the three day appointment wait in 2007 or the new procedure instead of radiation.

June 27th 2007, is a day I will not forget. We were at camp and that day was cold and drizzly. We had a fire going in the cook stove. Every spring as soon as the snow goes away, I get cut firewood for the camp. I fill the camp with wood, behind the stove, under the table, under the counter, in the porch and next to the fridge. When anyone asks why I just tell them it's to make room for the green wood in the lean-to. But the truth is that I don't want to go to the wood pile in the summer because snakes like wood piles.

It was late afternoon and I was puttering around in the shed, when I heard Verna call, "Vic, come here". I went and asked what she wanted. She said, "There's a snake behind the stove". I looked and sure enough it was lying on the top of the wood soaking in the warmth of the stove. There was a long handled spade shovel outside the door but I was reluctant to use it on the snake in case I missed the first jab. So I got my trusty twelve gauge and told Verna to take our dog Tippy into the porch. I loaded the gun, aimed and fired. When the smoke cleared there was no sign of the snake. The wall was peppered with pellets. The electric coffee percolator sitting on the counter was peppered with blood. We found about four inches of the tail end lying on the chair and Verna found part of the head on the floor when she was cleaning up.

Sweating and shaking, I wondered if I would be able to go under the covers and sleep that night, thinking perhaps the snake had a brother or relative inside the camp some place. However, when time came I was surprised that I was able to go to bed and fall asleep with no problem. Why, I wondered, did the Higher Power create such a situation? Was it to keep me from getting to complacent and to remind me the Power is still there? I was also provided with enough courage to survive living in the cabin with no other thoughts of the snake.

There are a lot of improvements around the camp. From the old Coleman lantern to propane lights, or electric lights from the generator, even a microwave. Now I cook meals at home, fill plastic containers, freeze them bring them to camp and when supper time comes, all I have to do is pop a container in the microwave oven and in ten minutes dinner is served. As opposed to the earlier days when I would come home to camp tired and have to start a fire, peel potatoes and cook supper. This way is so much better and quicker.

In 1995 I was able to operate a radio phone. I could call home or the wife could call me. In 1999 I purchased a satellite phone which was portable so I could call anywhere at any time. In the evenings I can listen to a satellite radio with no commercials. The t.v and its "call now", I'm glad to get away from.

While searching for my trapping diaries I came across a history book of my home town in Saskatchewan, published in 1984. I read some histories of some families and it made me aware of the tremendous changes in life style. I mentioned the change in lighting from the Coleman lantern. I still remember my parents and I using a kerosene lamp which lighted a small area around the table, but the corners of the room were still dark.

I find myself sort of in the middle seeing as how I can relate to the horse and buggy days. My parents would not have been able to comprehend the technology of today. Imagine them getting money out of a wall from something called an ATM or trying to understand space travel, satellites, cell phones, computers and television just to name a few. And the mode of travel at the present time, four wheels instead of four legs and flying in jets to get to a place in hours rather than days or months.

The young generation takes today's technology for granted. They would not be able to imagine the lives of the pioneers where everything was done by hand. Plows and wagons were pulled by people before the started using oxen (neutered male cattle). Today it's a big deal just to get them to take out the garbage, and what would they do without their cell phones attached to their ears or their instant messaging on the computer.

This is my second attempt at writing this book. The first version I completed and sent to the publisher and things didn't work out the way I expected, so I started having doubts as to whether or not it was worth pursuing.

I decided to get an outside opinion. Larry, from a Sarnia Radio station agreed to my read my book and to give me his honest opinion. So I packed the book, pictures and all and enclosed a paid postage return envelope and entrusted the parcel to Canada Post. It never reached Sarnia, don't know why but it just disappeared into thin air.

I was about to give up the whole idea, but then I started telling some people about my attempt at writing a book and what it would entail and they were all very encouraging. After thinking it over I decided that I would give it another try. Now as I am nearing the end of my book, I believe the loss of the first version was a blessing in disguise. This one is just about twice the length of the first one, which means I had left out a lot of information that should have been included. I just wanted to put on paper my experiences, mostly to relate the actions of the Higher Power that had on the outcome of my life.

Despite the lack of planning in my life, things happened due to destiny or a master plan unknown to me. I don't know or understand it but I gratefully accept it.

I can compare my life to a piece of driftwood on the river of life, sometimes getting snagged then getting loose again, but always moving. Someday I'll get water logged and sink out of site.

20

Healthy Recipes

I attended a pancake breakfast about twenty years ago in Manitoba. The pancakes that were served were very tasty. I asked for the recipe and was then shown a bag of mix they used. I was made at Robin Hood Flour Mills in Saskatoon, using whole wheat flour and before heading home I purchased a case. Sharing them with friends and relatives it didn't last long. The cost of shipping from Saskatoon was too expensive, so I looked at the list of ingredients on the bag and decided to try to make my own mixture.

My daughter and I began to experiment with ratios of ingredients. After numerous attempts, we were able to come up with just as good, if not better that the original. I still make and enjoy these pancakes and want to share my recipe with you.

Whole Wheat Pancake Mix

2 cups whole wheat flour
2 cups barley flour
4 tsp. sugar
2 tsp. salt
8 tsp. whey powder (level)
8 tsp. baking powder (level)
8 tsp. wheat germ (heaping)
8 tsp. wheat bran (heaping)

Mix all ingredients well.

Pancakes

1 cup pancake mix
1 cup water
1 tbsp. oil

1 beaten egg

Mix well and make in a frying pan or grill. Works well in waffle iron.

Flax Cookies

1¼ cup whole wheat flour
½ cup rolled oats
1/3 cup ground flax
¼ cup whole flax
½ tsp. salt
1 tsp. baking soda
1 tsp. cinnamon
½ cup mashed ripe banana
½ cup brown sugar
1 egg beaten
2 tbsp. molasses
1/3 cup oil

Mix the first seven ingredients. In a separate bowl beat the last 5 ingredients. Add dry mixture and stir well. If the batter is too soft add ¼ cup of wheat germ. Drop by spoonfuls on greased cookie sheet and flatten with a fork. Bake in a 325 degree oven for 25 minutes. Cool on wire rack. Store in refrigerator in and open container for crispy cookies and a closed container for soft cookies.

Date Cookies

1 cup chopped dates
½ cup shelled sunflower seeds (chopped if desired)
1 cup oatmeal (rolled oats)
½ cup wheat germ
1/3 cup oil
1 tsp. vanilla

Mix all ingredients together. If the batter is too soft add more wheat germ. Drop by spoonfuls on an oiled cookie sheet and flatten with a fork. Bake 20 minutes in a 350 degree oven. Cool on a rack.

Whole Wheat Pie Crust

11/3 cup whole wheat flour
1 tbsp. white sugar
1 tsp. baking powder
¼ tsp. salt
½ cup non hydrogenated margarine
4 to 6 tbsp. ice water

Mix together dry ingredients. Cut in margarine to make coarse crumbs. Add ice water 1 tbsp. at a time, just so the dough holds together. Divide dough in half. Shape into a ball and flatten between two sheets of floured waxed paper. Roll out to slightly larger than the pie plate. Remove top wax paper; place the pie plate upside down on the dough. Slide a piece of cardboard under the wax paper and invert right side up. Peel off top wax paper. Makes two single pie crusts.

Biscuits

21/2 cups whole wheat flour
½ tsp. salt
1 tbsp. baking powder
1 tsp. cinnamon
½ cup milk
1 egg
4 tbsp. honey
¼ cup non hydrogenated margarine
(Optional) I apple peeled, cored and finely diced
1/3 cup raisins

Combine dry ingredients in a bowl. Cut in honey and margarine to make coarse crumbs. Beat the egg in the milk. Add to dry ingredients to make soft dough. Knead 8 to 10 times, flatten or roll out to ½" thickness. Cut with cookie cutter or pizza cutter. Bake 15 minutes in a 400 degree oven on a greased (lightly) cookie sheet. Cool on a wire rack.

Birdseed Squares

11/2 cup chocolate chips
½ cup peanut butter
½ cup sesame seeds

½ cup shelled sunflower seeds (chopped if desired)
½ cup pumpkin seeds
½ ground flax
½ cup coconut
½ cup wheat germ
½ cup wheat bran
¼ cup hemp seeds
¼ cup oil

Combine and mix well all dry ingredients. Add ¼ cup oil. In another bowl melt chocolate chips and peanut butter, stir. Add the other ingredients and mix well. Pour into a 9 x 13" well greased pan. Press down evenly with a sprayed spatula. Cool in the refrigerator over night. Cut into desired squares.

Bannock

This recipe came in handy when I ran short of bread at camp.

2 cups whole wheat flour
1 tsp. salt
3 tsps. baking powder
¼ cup non hydrogenated margarine
¾ cup water

Mix together to make a soft dough. Pat into an oiled cast iron fry pan. Fry each side for 15 minutes on medium heat or bake in a 450 degree oven for 20 minutes. Will also work on a campfire using moderate heat.

978-0-595-47219-2
0-595-47219-2

Printed in the United States
124331LV00002B/6/P